IT ALL STAR
BILLIE H⸺DAY

A Memoir of Jazz

Gene Chronopoulos

iUniverse, Inc.
New York   Bloomington

iUniverse books may be ordered through booksellers or by contacting:

iUniverse
1663 Liberty Drive
Bloomington, IN 47403
www.iuniverse.com
1-800-Authors (1-800-288-4677)

Because of the dynamic nature of the Internet, any Web addresses or links contained in this book may have changed since publication and may no longer be valid. The views expressed in this work are solely those of the author and do not necessarily reflect the views of the publisher, and the publisher hereby disclaims any responsibility for them.

ISBN: 978-1-4502-0671-6 (sc)
ISBN: 978-1-4502-0670-9 (ebook)
ISBN: 978-1-4502-0669-3 (dj)

Printed in the United States of America

iUniverse rev. date: 04/20/2010

Layout Design by James Kronos

"For Gene … Stay as fine as you are …Billie Holiday"

Dedication

This book is dedicated to Louis Armstrong, Duke Ellington, Dizzy Gillespie, Charlie Parker, Teddy Wilson, Lester Young, and, of course, Billie Holiday.

And to all of the magnificent musicians who made America's name glow throughout the world.

It All Started with Billie Holiday

It was summer. It was hot. It was muggy. And it was one of those New Hampshire nights when all the mosquitoes in the New England area came to Manchester, where I lived, just to bite me. Needless to say it was the kind of New England night that I loved. We lived in a section of Manchester, which was primarily Greek but also included Polish, Irish, and two Portuguese families, while we were surrounded by French Canadians who used to tell us that we'd go to "ell" (the English "hell") because I wasn't "catolik" (the English "Catholic"). They also were the majority ethnic group in the city. So I learned some French. Also, close to the Greek section, there were many Syrians and Armenians.

Growing up in this area was more European than American. That is not to say that we didn't assimilate. In fact, statistics show that Greeks assimilate into the American culture faster than other ethnic groups. We were Greek at home where we spoke Greek because our parents wanted us to be ready when we went back to Greece, which all Greeks who came here in the 30s planned to do. Our Easter was different, we had red eggshells all over the sidewalks, we celebrated name days rather than birthdays, but we still looked like everybody else. Fortunately, the Jewish kids had their holidays and special occasions so it was not bad at all. At best, it was learning about people and their cultures for the ones that were "only" Americans.

When one of the Greek mothers baked a Greek pastry that was special she would send some around the neighborhood to her friends. On this one particular evening, my mother had made a Greek pastry for which she was justly well known. Being the youngest of four children,

I was elected, as usual, to make the delivery. I wasn't too happy about this because at the age of eleven or twelve, I think you can imagine the solid date I had that night. But, I went anyway. I was going to Mrs. Gianakis' house.

I took the dessert and hurried to her house. I climbed the squeaking stairs to the third floor and knocked on the door. Mrs. Gianakis' daughter, Vasso, opened the door, and with her left index finger held against her lips, motioned me to be quiet. With her right hand, she motioned for me to come in.

She was smoking a cigarette, which in the 1950s, Greek girls did not do. Or so they say. There was a gooseneck floor lamp behind the armchair in which Vasso was sitting. The neck of the lamp was high above her head with the smoke rising toward the ceiling and through the opening at the top of the lampshade. The smoke took on the color of the more orangey than amber lampshade, which gave the room an aura of exotic beauty. The phonograph was playing someone singing the words, "My life a hell you're making." That one line stuck in my mind because at the time, I only knew American pop music of "moon, June, spoon, croon." Those were little ditties...whereas the Greek music I grew up with was all about life, death, joy, love and tragedy.

So when I heard "hell" I guess it struck a chord in my Greek heritage. I started to speak and Vasso said, "Shhh". And so we listened to it and when it was over I said, "Who is that?" She responded, "Billie Holiday." I told her, "I want to hear it again." *Body and Soul* was the song and she played it again. This time I was jazzed by "...what lies before me, a future that's stormy, a winter that's gray and cold, unless there's magic, the end will be tragic..." The feeling was alive with sadness. That moment has stayed with me for over fifty years. The feeling that Billie Holiday put into the song, was like nothing I had ever heard before that one single moment.

When I was about four years old, a neighbor would stand me on a table and tell me to sing and then she would give me some candy. Greek songs I had learned from my father, who played the bouzouki, were all I knew. I sang in the church choir and now I wanted to be a jazz singer.

Anyway, when I heard Billie Holiday singing, it changed my life and broadened my musical taste to the point that I wanted to learn who the musicians were and what kind of music this was. At the time, the change from 78s to LPs was going on. As fate would have it, I went down to the record store the next day looking for Billie Holiday records. Now remember, I didn't know anything about jazz. All I knew were the pop singers of the day. I learned these songs and sang them. So, I went to the record store and asked for Billie Holiday records. The lady asked if I wanted the LPs and I said I didn't have a player. She suggested I buy the 78s, which were on sale. Besides, she didn't have Billie on LP.

Behind the counter on the bottom shelf there were a bunch of albums full of dust. She said, "I have two Billie Holiday albums," and she gave me both to look at. Well, they were $1.98 each – now that's for four records for eight songs, which is like fifty cents a record. But when you bought them otherwise, it was normally something like eighty-nine cents or a $1.10 or something like that. They were re-issues on the Columbia label called "Hot Jazz Classics" with Teddy Wilson and "Billie Holiday Sings." Well, I bought them.

After that, all I did was play those records over and over. I learned the songs (all sixteen of them) and just loved the feeling and the backing. Then I started learning the musicians' names and their instruments. There were three songs that I knew from before, but she sang them differently: *Summertime, When You're Smiling,* and *I Can't Get Started.* To this day, only her versions of these songs seem right. Then I started to read and learn about improvisation and about the many singers she had influenced. She was the first really true modern jazz singer. She was the original.

Chapter 2

And so, for the next couple of years, I hounded magazine and record stores for anything by Billie Holiday. Unfortunately, I could find no books on jazz. There were only two record stores in town. There were two magazines. One was DOWNBEAT and the other was METRONOME. The latter became my favorite because they wrote about the new jazz called bebop. Later, it was simply called bop. It was too bad that people didn't understand the music because so many of us loved it. Barry Ulanov became my idol because he wrote so that even I could understand him. And he loved Billie Holiday. I couldn't afford to buy the magazines so I read them there in the store. But soon that came to an end. My father came to my rescue but he didn't know it.

He asked me to go help a Jewish couple that lived down the street from us because they were old. I was to go every Saturday. I did this and it was okay. He gave me some money, a buck or two, I don't remember because I didn't expect anything. When the winter months came, my responsibilities increased. It was getting darker earlier and I had to turn on the lights and light the potbelly black stove in the kitchen since it was also getting colder. I was getting irked with this and I told my father that Mr. Kaplan was lazy. Why couldn't he do anything? My father explained that the Kaplans were Orthodox and did not work on Saturdays for religious reasons. I told him that we were Orthodox too, but I had to work on Saturdays. He told me that the Kaplans were Orthodox Jews and that we were Greek Orthodox Christians. He said that the Jews were waiting for the Messiah for the first time and that we were waiting for his Second Coming. That was very logical to me. So, I continued helping the Kaplans. And I was looking for more work.

I don't know if I said anything to Mr. Kaplan or not but one day he offered me a job. He had a butcher shop and he lived upstairs from his shop. He wanted me to become a chicken plucker. He would slaughter the chickens and put them into boiling water and then I, while wearing rubber gloves, would take them out of the water and hang them on hooks. I would then begin plucking their feathers. I was amazed how fast it went. Once the feathers were plucked, Mr. Kaplan or his wife would hold them over an open flame to burn off whatever little feathers remained. And I got a dime a chicken. So my income was increasing. Ten chickens meant one record!

I was looking forward to buying some records that I had heard at the store. It was a time when you could listen to records before buying them. I was generally having a very happy life. I wanted to become a jazz singer. I asked the older guys in the neighborhood about Billie Holiday and they began educating me. They told me about the sidemen who worked with her on her various records; Lester Young, Roy Eldridge, Bunny Berigan, Artie Shaw, Benny Goodman, Buck Clayton, and of course the pianist, Teddy Wilson. There were dozens of others and each person had his favorites. I was reading METRONOME Magazine and discovering Dizzy Gillespie, Charlie Parker, Thelonious Monk, and many others. Initially, these were all merely names to me since I had heard so few of them on record. They were the giants who were continuing the logical evolution of jazz. Thinking back, I am amazed at the guys in Manchester knowing so much about jazz. By now, my ears were open to new sounds.

On a Saturday afternoon at the movies, I saw a short film on Count Basie with his small group backing Billie Holiday also called Lady Day, a name given to her by Lester Young. She in turn named him The President, which became "Pres" as Lady Day became "Lady". She sang *Now or Never* and *God Bless the Child*, both of which she had written. I was pinned to my seat. Other than a few pictures, this is the first time that I was seeing her "live". It was mesmerizing… the sound of her voice, her beauty, her hands, her fingers popping (snapping) and her genius for projecting the feeling of each song. (One must remember that in the thirties, when she was starting to create all those classic recordings, she was 22 years old. And they are as fresh today as they were then.)

♪

Chapter 3

When I went to high school, I found a new book about jazz by Barry Ulanov called *A History of Jazz in America*. Now I was able to talk to the older guys because the book explained the steps by which the different eras of jazz followed each other. One of the people I loved to talk to was a guy named Jimmy. I had met him in church. He wrote a music column for the local Sunday newspaper, which I read without fail. One day, I was walking by a shoeshine parlor and saw him sitting there getting a shine. I had read in DOWNBEAT that a critic reviewing a Billie Holiday recording wrote, "I'm afraid it's rapidly becoming 'Lady Yesterday'." I was so angry and wrote them a letter. It was never published. It was also at this time that I was enjoying the bop musicians and the singer who grew out of that school (along with Miles Davis) was Sarah Vaughn. She had the best voice in jazz and could have sung opera with her range. And she was a great jazz singer. Sarah was the favorite in many polls. Others loved Ella Fitzgerald.

So when I saw Jimmy in the shoeshine parlor, I asked him who the greatest jazz singer was and he told me Billie Holiday. I was so happy. Continuing his opinion he explained her problems with narcotics and said she had spent a year in jail for using narcotics. That was the first I knew of that and immediately erased it from my mind. I did not want to hear it. To this day, there is more talk about her addiction than about her genius. And that is ridiculous.

Jimmy invited me to his house to listen to some records (his mother being Greek fed us of course). It was then that I heard *How High the Moon* as a ballad by the Boyd Rayburn Orchestra with Ginny Powell singing. For two or three years before, we used to call it the national anthem of jazz. Everyone played it. It was one of my favorite Ella Fitzgerald recordings. He also introduced me to the bands of Jimmy Lunceford, Chick Webb, and the other big bands he loved.

At the time that I was discovering jazz, there was a great controversy over the validity of the bop movement and the innovators of the late forties and early fifties. I grew up musically with Lady Day, Pres, Charlie Parker, and Dizzy Gillespie whose music was all very exciting to my ears. In addition, Duke Ellington, Count Basie and Woody Herman were all absorbed into my heart and soul. That is when I decided that there wasn't a single era of jazz that I did not like. There may have been some individual players I didn't like but in general, I just loved jazz. Through Lady Day and Pres, I learned about the Basie band. Barry Ulanov taught me to love the music of Duke Ellington. But we were also listening to Woody Herman because his band was very popular at the time, which featured some extraordinary musicians.

Reading Barry Ulanov's book on jazz, I learned about four people whom he called "figures of transition." They were Lester Young, Roy Eldridge, Jimmy Blanton, and Charlie Christian. The tenor sax player, Lester Young, was one of the first to be called "cool". His followers were and are legion. It was said that Charlie Parker learned Pres' records note for note. Roy Eldridge's music was the foundation on which Dizzy Gillespie built his masterful playing as Diz himself has said. Jimmy Blanton was with Duke Ellington from 1939 to the early forties (the best band in the history of jazz for many years). Barry Ulanov wrote, "The bass was a thumper when he took over; he left it a jumper. Bass players all over America were won over with a couple of measures of *Jack The Bear*, *Ko – Ko* and *Sepia Serenade*, when they heard the tone and the authority and the beat of the best bass man jazz has ever known." He died at the age of twenty-three and his playing is still heard in bass players everywhere. And then there was Charlie Christian who played with so much innovation that he amazed all who heard him. And this was as early as 1939.

Charlie Christian played with the Benny Goodman Band, but there were jam sessions at a place in Harlem called Minton's Playhouse where Christian went to jam. Other jazz musicians who had new ideas would gather there to play, but Charlie was the one who made people stand around and listen to his innovations on guitar. His sound is still heard in many guitarists of today. Thankfully, some of the sessions at Minton's Playhouse have been captured on record. The "figures of transition" together with others, but especially Dizzy Gillespie and Charlie Parker, brought jazz to a new era called bop. Miles Davis, who had played trumpet with "Bird" (Charlie Parker) when Miles was only twenty, brought further innovations to jazz and continued to do so until his death in 1991.

Chapter 4

A few doors from the Kaplan butcher shop, there was a shop that shipped Greek feta cheese, olives, and olive oil, as well as other Greek foodstuffs around the United States. The owner's name was Niko. He had a farm in Vermont, which approximated the weather of his hometown in the north of Greece. He needed someone to pack the boxes for the orders, which were shipped around the country. He had seen me deliver the ACROPOLIS, a Greek language newspaper that my father wrote, on Saturday mornings and also running errands for the Kaplans. He also thought I was terrific as a chicken plucker. Mr. Niko asked my father if I could work as a shipping clerk. The pay was a $1.25 an hour. My father sent me to talk to him. He told me what he wanted and said that he would give me more when I learned how to do some of the other jobs. In time, because I read and wrote Greek, he sent me to a summer class to learn how to type. After that, I started reading the letters and writing the orders on the back of the envelopes. I then typed the shipping labels and after that I would go into the area next to the office to pack the orders. At four thirty, five times a week, the Turk (we called him that because his Turkish name was too difficult to pronounce) would come by and together we would load his pick-up and go to the post office to mail the packages. He always waited to take me home but in the warmer months I would tell him to leave and I would go across the street to a place called The Palace Drug to meet friends (the rich kids who didn't need to work) who congregated there after school or I would go to a record store, which was on the way home. To this day, I can get lost in bookstores or record shops for hours.

In a very short time (less than a year), I was doing it all but now for a $1.50 an hour. Business was really booming, and I was working more hours, so I was making more money. My record collection was growing. Notwithstanding the lack of time after school, I still had time to go to the Palace Drug and elsewhere where the jukeboxes were sadly lacking in jazz records. I started a campaign to get the owners of these places to put in some Ellington, Basie and Billie. Forget it. They just couldn't dig it. Thankfully, Billy Eckstine and Sarah Vaughn and others broke through into the pop market and we got to hear them on the jukebox. We tried to emulate the movies and their portrayal of teenagers of the fifties. I have to say that we were listening to better music to dance to because we were ordering R & B records that we heard on the radio from Baltimore and New York. Tiny Bradshaw, Wynonie Harris, Earl Bostic, Ruth Brown, Fats Domino, and other groups like that. We used these for dancing but we listened to bop. And I always listened to Billie.

I had seen ads in the music magazines about sides by Billie being available in New York from a man named Boris Rose. I wrote and ordered a couple of Billie Holiday records. Some idiot told me she had recorded a "dirty" song and therefore it was banned from the radio. So I ordered it. The records were on acetate so the sound was not good. And initially, I couldn't make out all of the lyrics.

On Saturday nights, there were dances at the "Y", which were heavily attended. There was a game room, a piano available for those who could play, as well as dancing to recordings in the dance hall. I took the record to the "Y" to play it at the dance. This was in keeping with the crusade I was on to make known the songs of Billie Holiday. I "premiered" the record there at the dance. It made no sense. It wasn't up-tempo for dancing. It was just slow. It was one of the few times that I had goofed. It wasn't titillating, and no one liked it. I took it home and played it there but it was badly recorded. I played it over and over and it began to have some meaning. I called up Jimmy and told him about it. He asked what it meant to me, and after clarifying a couple of words here and there, I told him what I thought it meant. He said, "That's what it is."

I went to the library and found nothing. I went to the record stores and asked the girl there but she didn't know. She called someone over and he couldn't explain it to me. So I went back to Jimmy for further explanation. It was *Strange Fruit*, a song that protested the lynching of blacks whenever some satanic maniacs wished to kill a black man. I don't think I can convey in words the feeling to this day that this song evokes, except to say that it's a cry for civil rights and you wanted to fight for those rights whenever you heard that song. I went home and played the record over and over.

It is important to quote TIME Magazine when they chose it as the "Best Song of the Century." They said, "In this sad, shadowy song about lynching in the South, history's greatest jazz singer comes to terms with history." On the flip side of the original, was *Fine and Mellow*, which was considered the A side upon its release in 1939. This is one of the few real blues that she recorded.

♪

Chapter 5

As stated before, the popularity of Sarah Vaughn and Billy Eckstine made listening to the radio much better. Also big was Nat King Cole with hits like *Too Young* and *Mona Lisa,* which were primarily vocals. Prior to this he would sing but also play great piano on things like *Route 66* and *Straighten Up and Fly Right*. I liked his singing but I was much more impressed at the time with four songs on two 12" recordings where he played piano with Lester Young and Red Callendar on bass. The tunes were *Indiana, Body and Soul, Tea for Two*, and *I Can't Get Started,* which are all masterpieces. As for Billy Eckstine, all my male friends and I wanted to dress like him with his famous "Mr. B" shirt collar. In the meantime, all the pictures of the white girls going crazy over Eckstine and his singing was causing quite a stir among the bigots. In addition to his great singing, Billy Eckstine will also be remembered for his great band, which lasted from 1944 to 1947. This band at various times featured musicians like Charlie Parker, Dizzy Gillespie, Gene Ammons, Fats Navarro and Miles Davis to mention just a few of the better known musicians. And today, it is all on CD for your listening pleasure!

We also got a band together, a "voice" band, meaning that we emulated instruments. We had a guy who sounded like a trumpet, another like a trombone, a piano and I was on bass. Only the drummer had sticks, which he played on the granite columns situated on either side of the entrance to the local park called The Common in New England. We had learned a song and sang it as we walked down the street. It was Earl Bostic's *That's the Groovy Thing* that was our biggest hit and we even got many requests to not sing it.

While getting whatever re-issued sides on Columbia that were available, I was buying the Decca sides that Billie had recorded. Songs like *You Better Go Now, No More, I'll Look Around, What Is This Thing Called Love* and *Porgy*, which at the time was the closest she sounded to the way she sounded in person. After her death, James Baldwin said, "Billie Holiday would have made a splendid if somewhat overwhelming "Bess", and indeed, I should imagine that she was much closer to the original, whoever she was, of this portrait than anyone who has ever played or sung it."

I kept looking at 78s since they were still available. The record store that carried METRONOME Magazine brought in an album by Billie Holiday on four 78s on the Commodore label. I was thrilled. I thought that they were new releases and I flipped. There were two girls who wrote the recorded reviews for the school paper and I asked them if I could write a column. They agreed and I include it here to show you how dumb I was. The recordings were from 1939 and 1944 and I thought they were new in the fifties.

Platter Patter

"Ready to dig dat disc and get hip with some more favorite spinners? Okay, then, for those of you who enjoy hearing the great voice of Billie Holiday, give a listen to *You're My Thrill*. By changing a few notes here and there, adding her own words, and striking unexpected notes with her curiously husky voice, Billie makes a classic out of every one of her recordings. Listen to the *Queen of Torch Songs* make classics of *Lover, Come Back to Me, I Cover the Waterfront*, and the other recordings included in her new Commodore album.

Another top singer (who has been tops for 17 years), Ella Fitzgerald, offers *It's Too Soon to Know*, a beautiful ballad and *Flying Home*, the reverse of which is *Lady Be Good*, two outstanding bop vocals welcome in anyone's record collection.

Sarah Vaughn, a vocalist who has taken her place alongside Billie and Ella, has waxed *Summertime* and *Don't Worry 'Bout Me*. On the latter, pay special attention to the marvelous piano backing of Teddy Wilson. Another top vocal disc is *I'll Remember April* by June Christy.

Duke Ellington's blind singer, Al Hibbler, gives his all to *Danny Boy* and *Trees*, two very inspiring numbers. So much for the vocal side of music. Let's switch to the instruments.

George Shearing's *I'll Remember April* and *September in the Rain* are two of his best recordings. Lester Young, President of the tenor sax men, really jumps on *Jumping with Symphony Sid*. Another top tenor man is Gene Ammons, and he proves this with his smooth recording of *La Vie En Rose*, *My Foolish Heart* and *Goodbye*.

We're sure these songs will keep your head spinning for a while, anyway, so we'll close here by reminding you to note *Be My Love* by Mario Lanza.

(No, the last paragraph is not mine but commercialism always rears its ugly head).

Chapter 6

A short time later, I read in the Boston paper that Billie was performing at a club called the Hi-Hat. I decided to go. It was on a Saturday night. I finished my work at the cheese shop at about 1 P.M. and went home. I called my friends and told them that I was not going to the dance at the "Y". And I told my parents I was going to the dance at the Y but that would be after the birthday party I was going to at about 6 P.M. My brother Yanni was working so I took his gray striped suit, one of his ties and my own shoes. I did have to fold the sleeves on the jacket because they were too long. I went to the Greyhound bus depot and took a trip to Boston. It was about a two-hour ride to Boston. I got there about 8:30 and walked to the Hi-Hat after learning it was not too far away. (I was saving money.) Walking, I found out that it was far, but in those days we walked everywhere so it didn't bother me. When I got there, I put a cigarette into my mouth, but I did not inhale. (I said that first.) It was very dark. The club was upstairs and the waiting lounge was downstairs on the street level. It was packed but because I was only one person they promised me I'd get in. I thanked them. They never asked me anything else. So I was swinging.

I kept the cigarette hanging from my mouth, hunched my shoulders and walked very coolly away to a darker corner so that no one would look at me too closely. I waited there for the first show to end and the second show to begin. In about fifteen minutes or so, the first show let out and for another fifteen minutes, I was waiting and looking around at the crowd. Then I saw her. BILLIE HOLIDAY IN THE FLESH! I guess the dressing rooms were on the first level. I really didn't know where she came from but there she was. I went up to her and started talking to her and told her how much I loved her singing, how terrific I thought she was, which records of hers that I had, why I loved a particular phrase, and of course how I first heard the line in *Body and Soul* when she sang "my life a hell you're making" and how it was like hearing the songs from Greece that my father played on the bouzouki about trouble and love. She talked to me as if we were old friends, which really impressed me because in those days (or so I thought) celebrities were just not responsive to a young person.

She opened the kitchen door and leaned on it to keep it open, while she picked pieces off a ham that was there on the table. She just kept picking and eating pieces while she talked and she said, "I love ham. Only my mama used to make it like this and this is how I like it." We talked about a variety of things: jazz singing, music and songs. It was a wonderful and unforgettable experience. Then it was time to go to the show room. So up I went. It wasn't a big club, but that made it more intimate and better to see the artist up close.

The first song she sang, beginning with the verse was, *I Cover the Waterfront* and I went crazy. I'll never forget it. She sang some other songs that I was aware of but she didn't sing any of the songs recorded on Decca, except for *Don't Explain*.

After the show, I asked her if we could take a picture together and we did. You know the kind I mean, the nightclub photo kind that I got within a couple of hours. I went home very happy. I had to make copies of that picture because everybody wanted one. In fact, a friend of mine used to carry that picture around with him in his wallet for years. When he came to visit us here in California about 20 years later, he said, "Look, I still have that picture of you and Billie Holiday in my wallet." The edges were all worn out. We used to call him "Spider" because he danced like a spider with arms and legs going all over the place. But he loved dancing and jazz. And he was a pal.

When I got home it was 1:00 A.M. and my parents were frantic but they soon calmed down and my brother never complained about my wearing his suit. He was the quiet one in the family, but with a sense of humor that rocked. You can bet he took the suit to the cleaners the next day because it reeked of tobacco. He hated the smell and never smoked in his entire life. I didn't smoke the time I wore his suit, but unfortunately, I started to smoke a few years later, but no more.

A few months later, Billie was back at the Hi-Hat. My friend Joe had a rumble seat car, which was a 1930 yellow DeSoto Roadster with black fenders. Four of us went to Boston to see her. Joe was sixteen and had a license so he drove us down. When we got to the club they looked at us strangely but I started talking about Billie as if we were old friends. I showed the guy my picture with Billie. I guess he thought we were cool. If they carded us, we would say we forgot our IDs at home and drink soda. Or as we called it in New Hampshire: "tonic." What did we care? We came to hear the music anyway. Who knew about drinking? I was learning to drink responsibly at home. Every Sunday at the family dinner, my father would give us a drop or two of wine in a wine glass filled with water.

Chapter 7

In my third year of high school, when I was class president, I got up the courage to ask my two class advisors if I could put on an assembly on the history of jazz. To my surprise they said yes. I was surprised because these assemblies we had were concerned with teen issues, seminars or discussions about where we were heading in life. It always had a teacher involved as a supervisor. I guess they trusted me because they made me responsible for the rehearsals after school hours. The janitor would open the door and shortly after would leave. All I had to do was turn off the lights and close the door of the auditorium, which locked automatically. I was personally responsible for everything and anything at all for the privilege of putting on my "History of Jazz in America."

I called my friend Joe, who had the yellow DeSoto with the rumble seat. I wanted him to help me get musicians since he was in the band and played alto sax. "Let's put on a show (in the garage as Mickey Rooney and Judy Garland did)." He got a trumpet, a trombone, a tenor sax, piano, bass and drums with Joe on alto sax of course. And we were swinging. We started with *St. Louis Blues*, then a New Orleans number, followed by *I'm Coming, Virginia* Chicago style, hit some of the big band era stuff like *Don't Be That Way* and *Stomping at the Savoy,* and ended with a bop number. Interspersed we had three singers. I was the MC and explained that we were doing a "tribute" to the greats of jazz. I also explained that we couldn't do all of them - there were just too many. The first vocalist did Lee Wiley's *Someone to Watch Over Me* (but we couldn't get Maurice to accompany her). The great Fats Waller wanted so much to work with Lee Wiley and since he was under contact to RCA he used the pseudonym "Maurice" and played organ to her wonderful rendition of *Someone to Watch Over Me*. It's a classic record.

Our second vocalist did Sarah Vaughn's *Trouble Is a Man* and the third singer did Ella Fitzgerald's *How High the Moon*. The kids all loved it and asked us to do more assemblies like this. Where was the tribute to Billie Holiday or Duke Ellington or all the other giants? It was all verbal during introductions to the various segments. I had dreams of growing up to do something for jazz. I did nothing except make dozens of tapes to introduce my friends to my jazz favorites. And they are much happier than they were before they listened to these tapes. Recently, I introduced someone to the music of the Marsalis clan. He was so taken with the music of trumpeter Wynton Marsalis that he went out and bought everything that Wynton had ever recorded, both jazz and classical. He also bought most of Brandon Marsalis' CDs, on tenor sax. Of course, you know that I hate him. I could never afford to do that. I do have a fantasy though. One day, I want to be able to walk into a record store and pick out anything and everything I want.

In my senior year and still president, I got up the nerve and asked our class advisors if I could utilize the gym during the second to last period when it wasn't being used as a sock hop area for dancing. We would protect the gym floor by wearing only socks. Again, they agreed and even supplied me with a phonograph because it was for the school. I brought in a lot of Rhythm and Blues records and other records for dancing. For the lovers, I also brought in some Billie Holiday like *You're My Thrill, Crazy He Calls Me, Lover Man,* and things like *Them There Eyes* and *All of Me*. Everyone didn't fall in love dancing to Billie Holiday nor did everyone like the records. But, at that age to get a girl in your arms for a slow dance you'd listen to a dog howl. As it was, many liked Billie and if there was ever any question about how I felt, in our graduation yearbook, I named Billie in the "Idol Column". And no one ever asked me, "Who is Billie Holiday?" Only one friend said that I should not name a woman as my idol. I told him that I wanted her spiritual, human and musical attributes, not her physical ones. Blinders!

Most of the people that I went to school with were jazz fans. One of my best friends, Billy, was the star athlete of New Hampshire. It was a thrill to watch him play, especially basketball. With all of the activity in his life, he still had time for jazz. He decided he wanted to play tenor sax, so he bought one and started playing. He lived in a big house with four siblings and his mother, so it was hard to find a place to practice. He ended up practicing in the cellar near the heater. Unfortunately, the heating vents carried the sound of the sax into all the rooms. Despite all the complaints from his family, he would not give it up, but continued playing. The only free hours he had to practice were a little before and a little after midnight. That left his family with many sleepless nights. In time of course, he was forced to quit.

During my senior year, Billie came to sing at a club in Boston called Frolics. I tried to get people to go but to no avail. After a while, my sister said that she and her boyfriend would take us down. This was a different kind of club in terms of being a jazz club. The whole front of the room, which we were facing, was an elegant white curtain from ceiling to floor. When they announced "Ladies and Gentlemen, the Frolics is proud to present the great Lady Day, Miss Billie Holiday" the curtain went from the right to the extreme left and out came Lady Day all in white. It was very classy. Let me say now that Lady Day is the most beautiful woman I have ever seen. She never looked less than fabulous. Her warmth shone through at all times. But this time there was something special in her appearance and performance.

By this time, I was aware of most of the songs that she sang. She always said that she could never sing the same song the same way twice. The more I saw her, and the more I heard, confirmed it was absolutely true. I would hear a song that she had recorded and when I heard her sing it in person it was always different than the record. When the set was over, we went backstage to see her. There was a huge crowd there so we had to wait. It took about a half an hour but we waited. When we finally got into her dressing room, we stayed and talked for a long time. Two of the people with us had heard her for the first time that night. When we asked for an autographed picture, they said, "Can we have one too?" So we all got a picture. She was so friendly, we all stayed to talk with her a while longer. I told her I would be going to Los Angeles and she said that she was coming to Los Angeles in a few months and said, "Look me up, honey." I told her that when I see or hear that she's in Los Angeles, I'd be there. It was like a date.

Chapter 8

A couple of months later, school was out and within three weeks I was in a car on the first leg of my trip to California. Yanni, the younger of my two brothers, and my sister Kiki each gave me $50. A friend of mine named Flo was driving to Cleveland to visit her sister and offered me a ride. When we got to Cleveland I took a bus to Chicago and when I got to Chicago, I called my cousins. I still had my original $100. My friend Flo didn't ask for gas money, which most people were doing in those days, and the two meals we had were on her. The trip was a matter of hours but I will never forget her kindness and generosity. We are friends to this day and just recently, she hosted a class reunion for the few people from New Hampshire who now live in California. On the trip, we translated Greek love songs into English and the time passed beautifully. Her mother was with us and didn't dig the English lyrics to the Greek songs, but she sang along in Greek anyway.

The exciting thing about my trip to Chicago was that I knew that I would find a greater selection of jazz records there than in New Hampshire. Once in Chicago, the only thing I had in mind was to get to the jazz record shop, which was called the Blue Note Record Shop on 135 East 51st Street. While my relatives were at work, I got on the phone and called the record shop. I got directions as well and asked which bus to take and off I went. When I got home, my cousin asked me where I went. I told her that I had found the record shop I wanted and that I had found three Commodore discs that I didn't have. (By this time I knew that the Commodore sides were not new).

I remember also buying the four-record album set on Decca that I also didn't have called *Lover Man*, which was her one big hit. In those days the listing of discs by various artists only listed the latest releases. I also remember that there were no liner notes on the inside cover. When I got to California I copied them from a borrowed album. I found it strange that the liner notes were never printed. It was just a blank inside cover. I think now that it was probably because they were not spending too much money advertising her records. I bought *As Time Goes By* on the Commodore label and to this day, after hearing it by dozens of other singers, it's still Lady Day that surpasses all others. *I'll Be Seeing You*, which is also on Commodore and recorded in 1944, is the greatest version of a song sung by so many during World War II. Even though it was written in 1938, it became the perfect song for the couples and families who were parting for the duration of the war or worse. Billie's version is so moving you know the separation is going to be sad but with a lot of hope for a reunion. (Many years later, while viewing a documentary on television, the screen was filled with soldiers boarding a troop transport ship headed overseas. Her version of *I'll Be Seeing You* was used on the soundtrack and the visuals took on an added dimension of sadness. With Billie's vocal, it meant so much more.)

Finally, one cousin told me that I could have gotten killed in the neighborhood to which I had gone. I asked why and she said because blacks do not want whites in their neighborhoods. I was embarrassed that my cousin felt that way. So, I said coolly, "Well, I was so happy to be going to find some records that I loved and the guys in the record store were so cool and surprised that someone so young knew so much about jazz. I was very proud about that. We had a great talk. And when I left and went walking to the bus stop, I was so happy and smiling as I walked down the street that everyone was smiling back at me. I guess it's all attitude. Besides, what did I do that they should want to kill me? End of conversation. We played the records and it was the end of a beautiful day. It was also so good to talk to some intelligent people, like the guys at Blue Note. I didn't meet many of those kinds of people on my way to Chicago.

I stayed in Chicago for only nine or ten days because I was anxious to get to Los Angeles. Vasso's family had moved to Colton, which is outside of San Bernardino, about eight months earlier and I planned to visit them but first I had to go to Salt Lake City to see my Uncle Gus. My uncle and my mother had not seen each other for over thirty years before he came to see us a couple of years earlier in New Hampshire. His wife had died about a year before I got there so he was lonely. He wanted me to stay there, to send me to college but there was no way I would change my plans. Before leaving, I swam in the Great Salt Lake and about a week and a half later I took a train to San Bernardino.

Chapter 9

I guess it was about two days before I got to Vasso's house. She and her parents were living in the house of her uncle, her father's brother. He had been in Colton for twenty years and he lived in what looked like three small homes stuck together. Vasso and I began calling the house "the chicken coop". There were three bedrooms, a kitchen and a living room. Vasso worked at night at Norton Air Force Base and slept during the day. So I slept in her bed at night since there wasn't enough room. We had lots of laughs before she went to work and it was a nice vacation. Her parents wanted me to stay but I was in a hurry to get to Los Angeles. I now had $25 in my pocket. I did stay in Colton for a week and then I went to Los Angeles with a friend of Vasso's who was in the Air Force at Norton.

One night just before turning off the radio, I heard a record by Billie Holiday that I had never heard before. It was *Any Old Time* with the Artie Shaw Orchestra, the only record she ever made with him. I had heard so many radio shows with not one jazz station and then I heard Billie. I called the station and found out it was a jazz station. Surprise! Surprise! That was the station that Vasso listened to at work because they only played jazz from midnight to 6:00 A.M. Billie's Decca contract had run out and after that she had no recording contract. The last few records for Decca were getting released two by two and the radio stations were also playing the Columbia sides from the 40s.

I had called my Uncle Harry earlier that week. He told me to call him when I got to Los Angeles and to come soon. He was a sweet guy who spoke something like Mr. Magoo, but he didn't fool anyone. His family and my mother's family lived next door to each other in Greece and were very close. I got a job at the Ontra Cafeteria on Wilshire Boulevard in the Miracle Mile. Uncle Harry said I was to get a job where I could eat. That was most important. Then he said, "You will live with Steve and you will save your money." I listened to my uncle and took the few clothes I had and moved in with my cousin Steve. During this time Steve was looking very uncomfortable. When Uncle Harry left, I told Steve that I didn't have to live with him if there was going to be a problem, but Steve said there was no problem and that he had room. Steve was living with a beautiful redhead who was half Cherokee Indian. Her name was Sunny. He told me not to say anything to Uncle Harry. So naturally, there was no reason to tell Uncle Harry anything. Steve and Sunny ran a small neighborhood lounge at the corner of Kenmore and Third Street, just four blocks away from the Coconut Grove, which was in the Ambassador Hotel on Wilshire Boulevard.

Steve and Sunny were very good to me. She did all my laundry and they never let me spend a dime. I worked six days a week and my day off was Monday, which was also Steve and Sunny's day off. They would take me along for Mexican food and then to a movie on most of those Mondays. On my way home from work, I would stop by the bar to let them know that I was fine.

In the lounge, there was a wall unit, which had a slot into which you would put a quarter and then speak into a microphone to speak to the girl who was taking the requests. One night, I stayed awhile and Steve gave me a quarter and I requested *Porgy* by Billie Holiday. Steve was surprised that I knew Billie, so he put some money in and asked for Charlie Parker's *Now's the Time*. Now it was my turn to be surprised. Then I asked for Woody Herman's *Four Brothers*. And we were on our way. We played this game almost nightly. Of course, he would give me quarters to make requests and I was embarrassed to take them. One night he explained to me that the quarters he gave me were "house" quarters. That meant that they were all marked with red nail polish and that the house got those quarters back when the collectors came around to collect the money in the machine.

I also discovered a jazz radio station that used to have programs where one would call in and identify the song or artist that they had just played to win some records. On one occasion, I won five records. One of these was Oscar Pettiford playing cello on *Perdido;* another was tenor man Flip Phillips with Machito on *Caravan* and *Flying Home*. The third was one by Machito with his Afro-Cuban Band playing *U-Bla-Ba-Du*. I don't remember the two others. They were all 78s probably because they were cleaning out their record library to make room for LPs. On another show, I won two tickets to the movie premiere of *Pete Kelly's Blues*, the movie that featured Peggy Lee and Ella Fitzgerald and jazz. So I got my first feel of Hollywood!

My brother, Yanni, came to Los Angeles a few months after I did. We had planned it and if we liked it we would move our parents out. All these plans didn't work out the way we planned them, but with the help of God, they did happen. He got a job at North American Aviation in Inglewood. We didn't see each other as much as we would have liked to, but he did visit frequently. He also loved Steve and Sunny and was happy that we had such cool relatives. A few months later he was drafted, and chose the Marines over the Army.

The owner of Steve and Sunny's bar was selling it and they were moving to Alhambra where they would run another lounge and bar. Before they left they got married and told Uncle Harry. All was O.K. Soon I had to find a new place to live. I liked the area that I lived in and wanted to stay there. Between Third Street and Wilshire Boulevard, which was four blocks south, there were no apartment houses; just large aristocratic houses that I thought were inhabited by rich families. Little did I know.

Chapter 10

I wanted to stay in the area if I could. The Brown Derby was just around the corner on Wilshire Boulevard. A few blocks west was the Wiltern Theater, which ran first-run movies. A groovy little restaurant called Ollie Hammond's was also on Wilshire between the Brown Derby and the Wiltern. Across from the Brown Derby was the Coconut Grove in the Ambassador Hotel. Best of all was that a jazz club called the Tiffany Club was on Eighth Street, two blocks south and three blocks west of Kenmore. I loved the neighborhood. There was also a little club called The Haig on the corner of Wilshire and Kenmore, which for almost a full year would play a major part in my life.

From Third Street, I walked four blocks south to Wilshire and took the bus to the Ontra Cafeteria where I worked. One day while walking up to Wilshire, I saw a "Room for Rent" sign in the window of a large, two-story house just off Sixth Street.

After work, I went to the house and Mrs. Gerard, the owner, showed me the room. I loved it. It had a huge double bed, big bureau and a huge closet. I was set. She liked me and she charged me only $10 a week. Happily, I walked down to the bar to see Steve and Sunny. I told them the story and they asked what I knew about the people who owned the house. I stopped and thought. I turned around and went back to the house. It was only three blocks away. I rang the bell and a young lady was there. I asked where Mrs. Gerard was and she told me that Mrs. Gerard was her mother and that she had told her about me already. Her name was Maggie and she lived with her husband, Tom, and their seven-year-old son on the second story in what was the original master bedroom. The opposite side of the second story had been turned into a small apartment. It consisted of a living room with a day bed, a bath and shower, a large bedroom that fit three single beds and a small kitchen. A law student, who was leaving at the end of the current semester, was renting this. As it turned out, we would soon be renting this when he moved out. That happened when my sister arrived in June. In the meantime, I was beginning to feel as if I had grown up in this neighborhood.

At that time, Los Angeles was not the city it is today. In the Fifties, it was really many neighborhoods most of which had wonderful eating places, nightclubs, and other fun places that made you feel as if you were living on a movie set. At the Brown Derby, I had the greatest buttermilk pancakes with fresh blueberries. Their Cobb Salad, which someone at the *Derby* had invented, was a sensation. Many performers from the Coconut Grove would eat there but mostly at dinnertime. Still, I saw many celebrities there at lunch. Also, the Hollywood stars of the 50s and 60s were for the most part very hip. Famous actors and actresses were like children before the likes of the giants of jazz. I saw this for myself when I went to see various jazz groups at The Haig. The celebrity filled audience was in awe of these giants. And they, being performers, were really the best audience.

Ollie Hammond's was open all night and they had the smallest steak in the world for ninety-nine cents. It was the size of a hamburger and served with onion rings, French fries, and a piece of fresh fruit and Jell-O. At the Wiltern Theater, I saw many celebrities in the audience. But my real joy came from the jazz artists around town, and yet, I still hoped for a career in film. But now that had changed. I wanted to be in jazz films to tell the various stories about jazz and its musicians.

Then it happened, the Tiffany Club had an ad in the paper that Billie was coming in to play the club. In the 50s, the jazz clubs were small and you could see the performers' faces and their expressions. And that was necessary with people like Billie because her greatness was to convey a story to you and you alone. The club would be filled six nights a week. Not as it is today with weekend-only performers. So you could go during the week when there were less people but still busy. It was easier to talk to the musicians. It was really one of the few times when jazz was supported. I called Vasso and told her that Billie was coming to

Los Angeles. She told me that she and a girlfriend, Mary, would come in on a certain night. We went on a weeknight because we knew that weekends would be impossible. There was a two-drink minimum and a small cover charge. The other group on the bill with Billie was The Wardell Gray Group with Chico Hamilton on drums. Wardell Gray was another Lester Young disciple but he became his own man and brilliantly so. I remember he played *Twisted*, which Annie Ross, the singer, had just written lyrics to and which was becoming big in the L.A. area. The group was superb.

Then Billie came on. The intro was the same – "And now ladies and gentlemen the great Lady Day, Miss Billie Holiday!" This was the fourth time I was seeing her in person and I was in heaven. She looked great, sounded great and sang a long set. The crowd screamed for more. She came back and did two encores: *Ain't Nobody's Business* and *Lover Come Back to Me*. She also announced that she would be recording some new sides for Norman Granz. That was cause for a major celebration. There was no word of a new contract so when we heard this Vasso, her friend, Mary, and I screamed for joy. We went "Dutch" because none of us could afford to pay for the other two. I tried to go backstage to see her but it was impossible. The crowds were heavy for the two weeks she was at the Tiffany. I could not afford to go back to see her a second time or every night as I wanted.

Chapter 11

About three months before I left New Hampshire I bought a ten-inch LP of eight songs by Billie and Lester Young from the late thirties and early forties. Every record was a thrill for me because you could never hope to hear Billie except after midnight on the stations from New York or Baltimore. I thought it would be a good idea to let the world know about Billie, at least the world of jazz that listened to those stations. So I wrote a long letter to DOWNBEAT. Here is my *long* letter mailed from Los Angeles:

Billie's Doux

Since I have been in Los Angeles, my greatest joy was seeing Billie Holiday…this Billie, who many refer to as a "new" Billie is not new at all…is the great lady who made classics out of any and everything she sang…

Follow Billie's career from her days with Teddy and Lester to the present day. In between all this time, you can get the history of jazz. From barrelhouse and blues to ballads and swing, she remains the greatest jazz vocalist of all time…ask the disc jockeys to play some of her great records…

Gene Chronopoulos
Los Angeles

I think you know that the three periods represent words not printed by the magazine. Strangely enough, what you read above represents less than a third of the original letter. I was trying to start a mass mailing campaign and they printed a sound bite.

It was around this time that I was going to various clubs that had piano bars and that wanted people to sing. I didn't do that for too long because all the people wanted to hear were clapping songs like *Deep in the Heart of Texas* and such. I sang *She's Funny That Way* and no one listened to me because they were too busy talking. One guy came up to me, gave me his card, and told me to call him to audition for some club dates around town. On one audition, I sang *Deep Purple* and *Body and Soul*. They loved me (they said) but I would have to take lessons from them. I was looking for a job where I could learn but I had no luck. First of all, I had no money and second, I only knew about eight pop tunes of the day, and that's all they wanted was pop tunes. So it was back to seeing three movies for fifty cents in downtown Los Angeles where I worked, instead of buying a drink at the piano bar. That helped me a lot to see what was happening in the film business.

It was just a while after that when I got a job in a discount house (my fourteenth or fifteenth job), which sold everything from jewelry to furniture. It turned out that there were about ten salesmen but Herb, the boss' son, was just a little older than me and we talked about different things. Of course, I was still the spokesman for jazz and Billie Holiday. It turned out that Herb too was a jazz fan. It was so good to have someone to talk to about jazz.

There was a Columbia Records distribution store a half a block away. The employees there shopped at our discount house and we gave them a larger discount. In exchange, they would sell us LPs with a discount. The latest issue of METRONOME had a record review by Barry Ulanov about two ten-inch LPs by Lee Wiley. One was a Vincent Youmans tribute and the other featured the songs of Irving Berlin. Ulanov raved about them, so off I went to the Columbia distribution store. They gave me both for a mere $5. Ulanov was right. These were great sides. Some quibbled over the two-piano accompaniments and others loved it. It was a discovery of a great new jazz singer, at least for me. Prior to these two LPs, she had released another LP on Columbia entitled *Night in Manhattan* with Bobby Hackett on cornet (through him I discovered Bix Beiderbecke) and with Joe Buskin on piano. What an album! And I was unaware of it until I read the review of those two new LPs.

I got a raise and I still frequented used magazine and record stores. I picked up so many things. I was getting truly educated. I used to frequent Wallich's Music City in Hollywood. They allowed you to listen to records for free. I went almost two nights a week and spent a little time listening to the new jazz releases. I would go through the pages of METRONOME, DOWNBEAT, and other less significant publications and if I found Billie Holiday's name, no matter where I saw it, I would buy it. It was in the record store on Western and Hollywood Boulevard that I met this woman who knew Billie's records well and she touted me onto *Some Other Spring*. It was the beginning of my knowledge of Irene Higgenbotham, former wife of Teddy Wilson and a superb songwriter. This store had bins upon bins of 78s and I went through them all. I didn't buy much and it took me almost a year to find some gems.

The earliest clipping I found was the one in a 1939 issue of DOWNBEAT praising her recordings of *Easy Living, Foolin' Myself, Sun Showers, Yours and Mine, Without Your Love, Me, Myself, and I* with a picture of Billie. The caption read, "Billie Holiday: More good work with or without Teddy!" Teddy of course is Teddy Wilson, along with praises for Lester Young, Buck Clayton and Johnny Hodges among them. I had four of the six sides so my mission now was to get the two that I didn't have. *Sun Showers* and *Yours and Mine*. This was one of the ways I found out about various records. These did not become available for years.

From METRONOME, July 1943, a picture and a caption by Leonard Feather: "*As Time Goes By* Billie Holiday grows mellower vocally. Her version of the song by that name has been one of 52nd Street's biggest thrills lately." This is one of the records I bought in Chicago. I couldn't understand why it wasn't a big hit for her. In fact, until I bought the record, I didn't even know that she had recorded it. My searches produced most of her story up until 1947, which included her success in the concert halls of Philadelphia on February 13, 1946 and Town Hall in New York three days later. Then I also found articles about her drug addiction and her time in prison. She served nine months on a sentence of a year and a day. A triumphant return at Carnegie Hall.

Rave record reviews with a rating of "A" from METRONOME and five stars from DOWNBEAT. And the articles in EBONY, OUR WORLD, and JET with titles like: "I'm Cured For Good Now," "How I Blew A Million Dollars," and "Can a Dope Addict Come Back?" It told a lot but somehow it became fodder for the increased sales of magazines. They didn't say much about her genius. She still had her voice but only one or two critics stuck by her, notably Barry Ulanov and Nat Hentoff. There may have been a couple of others but the majority of the critics tried to bury her before her time. It started in 1950 when a DOWNBEAT critic wrote, "It is rapidly becoming Lady Yesterday". That may have sounded clever then but today we see it for what it is: a cheap, corny shot.

The greatest items that I found in my search of printed items on Lady were the 1944 to 1947 ESQUIRE Jazz Yearbooks. The 1944 magazine was unavailable but I found a small pocketbook size called the "Armed Services" copy. The others were large oversized magazines about ten by fourteen and just teeming with pictures and stories of jazz greats from the 1920s to the mid-forties. Billie Holiday was chosen singer of the year in 1944 and 1947. In 1945, she came in second to Mildred Bailey and in 1946 Mildred Bailey and Ella Fitzgerald tied for first place and Billie came in second. These yearbooks were exciting. I got caught up in the arguments as to who was better and who was coming up. There was a vitality and love for jazz in these ESQUIREs, which is sadly lacking today. Even though it is true that there is more being written today about jazz, sadly, the current pieces are mostly antiseptic and clinical. Many of the critics have no passion for the music. Whereas the 78s were limited to approximately three minutes of music on each side, today's musicians record on CDs, which allows them the freedom to truly create. Even so, too many of them repeat riffs over and over. The great musicians of the past could say more on a 78 record than some of the new musicians can say on a whole CD.

The ESQUIRE yearbooks had dozens of writers commenting on jazz from the earliest years. The cost of these gems was a mere dollar. If some magazines could do that today, it would help to raise the awareness of jazz, get rid of the pseudo and quasi-jazz artists and help turn jazz, America's only art form, into America's most popular music. It is a shame that jazz LP sales are less than five percent of total music sales today. And ESQUIRE also had concerts where the winners played and sang.

Many groovy sides were recorded during those four years. Many were on V-Discs, twelve-inch records that were sent to the troops overseas. Maybe that's why the guys in New Hampshire got so hip. They were in the Army or Navy and certainly were exposed to these V-Discs.

Chapter 12

I got many letters from my mother and father to come home. My mother finally decided to come out and see what this California was all about and why I was so crazy to stay. I told them to come and see. It was sometime in late fall when my mother came out. Vasso's brother and his wife were driving to Colton so they asked my mother to come with them.

One fine day while I was cleaning off a table, I looked up and there standing on Wilshire Boulevard was my mother with my Uncle Harry looking at me and smiling. I almost dropped the tray I was carrying. It was a great reunion. I took some time off and went to show my mother Hollywood Boulevard, Farmer's Market and various Hollywood landmarks. With Uncle Harry, we went to Marineland, which was on the Palos Verdes Peninsula. My mother started picking greens in the area, which had not as yet been fully developed. There were some greens that she hadn't seen since she was a little girl in Greece. She remembered their names as she picked them. When she saw trees laden with lemons and oranges at the beginning of winter, that was it. People were watching as she picked the greens and some even asked why. She said, "To eat." We got some very funny looks.

We stopped in Redondo Beach and bought some fresh fish and went to Uncle Harry's home and had a Greek Island dinner with fish, greens and garlic sauce (skordalia). We had a great time while she was here because my parents had a great sense of humor. The only sad part was that my mother did not get to see Yanni, my brother, because he had been sent to Europe.

When my mother went back to New Hampshire she was greeted by those famous New England winters. She was even more intent on moving to California. I told my mother to tell my father that he would not have to shovel snow anymore.

Since Yanni and I had agreed to go to California, my mother (while she was here) and I decided to have my oldest brother, Steve, come the following February and then my sister would come in June. We hoped that our parents would get here before Thanksgiving.

When my mother told my father that we were moving to Los Angeles he said, "I didn't lose any donkeys to go looking for them." Translation: "No way I'm leaving." He was very happy in New Hampshire. He had a good job. He wrote the Greek newspaper. He spent time with his friends in the Greek coffee house talking politics, playing cards and backgammon. Why would he want to leave?

My father was insistent! He said he was not going. To which my mother answered, "Well, you'll be here alone. Do you want that or do you want to go and be with your children?" So, daddy came looking for his donkeys!

Steve drove out to California and brought my record collection with him. Paradise revisited! We rented the apartment in front of the house facing Kenmore Avenue because the semester had ended and the law student vacated and Kiki was coming in June.

I was in heaven; I had my records. I was listening to Billie and Duke Ellington, Count Basie, Woody Herman and all their amazing sidemen, Billy Eckstine, clarinetist Buddy DeFranco, pianist and composer Lennie Tristano, guitarist Charlie Christian, pianist and composer Thelonious Monk, trumpeter Dizzy Gillespie, alto saxophonist Charlie Parker, bassist Charlie Mingus, tenor saxophonist Gene Ammons, drummer Cozy Cole, alto saxophonist Lou Donaldson, baritone saxophonist Dexter Gordon, vibist Lionel Hampton, and pianists Art Tatum, Earl Hine, Fats Waller, George Shearing, and Teddy Wilson among many others. It may sound like a lot but I only had about one hundred 78s and maybe twelve to fifteen ten-inch LPs. I can go to any of these records and play them and they are as good today, for me, as they were when I first heard them because aside from the music, they all bring back very happy memories.

One day, I bought Dizzy Gillespie's *Swedish Suite* and the flip side was *I Should Care* but it was weeks before I heard it. When I did, I discovered Johnny Hartman who remains one of my favorite singers. I wore out that record but I found another one for ten cents. One day, there was someone visiting and I asked him to get that particular record from the album so that I could play it for him. He held the album in such a way that the records slid down into their individual sleeves and when he turned the sleeves he broke off a piece of the record. As a result, when I played the record it started "…let it upset me" (as it did). But good news, because of CDs I now have, I believe, all the records he ever made, including *I Should Care* with Diz. And of course one of the greatest vocal albums in the history of jazz is the one he made with John Coltrane on tenor sax; McCoy Tyner, piano; Jimmy Garrison, bass; and Elvin Jones, drums.

Chapter 13

One day, I called home (we didn't have our own phone) and got the landlady. I asked to speak to my sister. She gave me a message from Kiki and then told me that a jazz musician just rented the bottom floor apartment. I never knew there was an apartment there. It was directly beneath ours. As you walked into the house, you went right into the living room from the foyer and then into the dining room, kitchen, etc., where the owner lived. When coming into the house, if you went left you went into the apartment of the jazz musician. I think that it was a bathroom and a combination of a den and a bedroom or a sunroom. We never knew it was there, we thought it was for storage. Of course, I was interested.

"What's his name?" I asked.
"I don't know," she said.
"What does he play? His instrument?"
"I don't know."
"What does he look like?"
"I don't know. Maggie rented it to him and his wife."

Whereas I was slightly interested thinking it was a local talent, now I was curious. I wasn't home. So how could I find out? I got on the bus and went home.

Going home on the bus that day, I was thinking of who the jazz player could be. When I got home I asked the landlady about the musician. She hadn't learned anything because he rented the apartment from Maggie. If I had somewhere to go at night after work, I would always call home first to see if the jazz musician had moved in. One night when I called, Mrs. Gerard said that he had moved in. She was driving me crazy! She did find out that he played the saxophone. I said, "Yeah, but what kind of saxophone?" She didn't know except that she remembers that it was a large saxophone. I thought it could only be Serge Chaloff, a baritone player from Boston. Hooray, now I had something. Is he black or white I asked and she told me he was white. No doubt it was Chaloff. Many jazzmen from the East were coming to Los Angeles to check out the scene. If I remember correctly, the "new music" was being reported prominently (and initially) by the critics on the staff at METRONOME Magazine. Mrs. Gerard told me that he was very tall and had beautiful red hair. "Gerry Mulligan?" Yes, Mrs. Gerard cried. I screamed that this is the guy who worked with Miles Davis in New York. They had started the "cool school" of jazz. (She didn't have a clue!) Also part of the group on various recordings were Kai Winding or J.J. Johnson on trombone. John Lewis or Al Haig on piano; Lee Konitz alto sax; Max Roach or Kenny Clark drums; Al McKibbon, Nelson Boyd, or Joe Shulman on bass. On some sides, they also added Bill Barber on tuba and Junior Collins on French horn. Most of these sides were recorded in 1949 and were the forerunners of what arranger Gil Evans, who was also involved with the above named musicians, would later produce with Miles Davis, which include classics like *Sketches of Spain, Porgy and Bess,* and *Miles Ahead.*

What a thrill. I couldn't wait to meet him. I can't remember how we met, but I did visit him in his apartment a few times. We discussed music and he told me all about working with Miles Davis in 1949 and how exciting it was.

Soon after that, we invited him upstairs for dinner. Kiki had Greek meatballs, mashed potatoes and Greek salad. I'm sure there was something else but I can't remember and we invited him and Carol to dinner. I do remember that my brother Steve was not home that night, probably because he was rehearsing with two new members of a vocal quartet he had organized earlier. This happened often. In the past, if the quartet had not become successful in addition to their becoming stars or millionaires in a very short time, one or two would quit and the rehearsals would start all over again.

So Gerry and Carol came upstairs. I had bought a portable record player from the discount store where I worked and I was playing my records. I remember playing Duke Ellington's *Main Stem* and then I played the flip side, which was *Johnny Come Lately*. I also remember hoping that Gerry would like my taste. I asked him what he thought and he said, "How can you go wrong with Duke Ellington?" I relaxed and continued to change the 78s and put them on one at a time. I waited to hear his comments about the sides I was playing. Again, I learned a lot. It was also this night when I surprised Gerry by playing a 78 for him which had the song *Yesterdays* with only Lee Konitz on alto sax and Miles Davis on trumpet. The flip side was *Duet for Saxophone and Guitar* with Lee Konitz on alto and Billy Bauer on guitar. These duets were recorded at the time when Lee Konitz was studying with Lennie Tristano along with Lester Young's disciple, Warne Marsh.

Kiki had invited him up to eat because the landlady had said that he and his girlfriend were having a difficult time of it (it wasn't his wife as she thought originally). That night proved to be the beginning of a great period in my life. I also had found a copy of Duke Ellington's *Jack the Bear* with Jimmy Blanton and he loved it. Another time we were eating omelets and Greek salad. That's all we had. It had to be on a Thursday because that's usually when we ran short of money. I had gone to see Gerry and Carol to invite them to dinner. I apologized because we were not having a better meal. He had an apple in his hand and he held it up and said, "It's a lot better than this." That was the night that he told us that he was getting a group together and making a demo. It would be as new and as exciting as the recordings in 1949.

Chapter 14

During the course of this period, when Gerry was recording with his group, we met Chetty Baker, as we called him, Art Pepper, Stan Getz, musicians from the Lighthouse in Hermosa Beach and Louis Armstrong. Except for Armstrong, everyone else came to see Gerry and I was always there asking questions. I grew very fond of Chetty and Art Pepper. Chetty was a very shy guy and Art talked about everything with the same passion with which he played his alto sax. That's why I always dug most jazzmen. For me, they were the best, always focused, sincere and forging ahead.

We were also meeting these people because Gerry would tell us where he was playing, and with whom, and he would tell us to come and support him. And we did. The night we met Louis Armstrong was when he was one of the guest artists at a dance in South Central Los Angeles. He was on stage and we were standing right up in front with his perspiration falling all over us. There were so many people behind us that we couldn't back up. So we rationalized and said, "It's OK, man. It's Satch. It's gotta be healthy!"

About two months later, Gerry came running up the stairs with a record in his hand. "Here it is," he said, "Our demo." All excitement and happiness. I played it for us to hear and then he said, "Keep it and listen to it again, and let me know how you like it, and which side you like best."

We felt so honored. Then he left. The first side was *Bernie's Tune* and the flip side was *Lullaby of the Leaves*. I don't remember which we liked best, but I can tell you that we knew we were hearing something very special. The blend of Gerry and Chetty was so cool. Gerry came up the next day and we discussed it. First of all, there was no piano. The sounds they created were so different. We loved both sides and he was thrilled. He was playing at various clubs around town and we went to a place in Hollywood just off Hollywood Boulevard on Vine Street. We were thrilled to go and hear the new tune he told us about. We went into the club and asked when the Gerry Mulligan Quartet would be on. We sat and waited. We ordered a drink, which was of course watered down. We didn't care because we were there to hear the music. Besides, none of us was old enough to drink except for my brother Steve, the athlete who didn't drink anyway. To make a long story short (we found out later), Gerry and the club owner had an argument and Gerry walked out. On his way out, he saw us and waved for us to follow him out. We got up, and on the way out, they tried to get us to stay but we said, "Oh, no. No. We came here for Mr. Mulligan," and ceremoniously walked out with heads held high.

Most club owners at the time didn't really treat new talent well. We witnessed many of such abuses. It didn't matter because in a very short time Gerry told us that he was opening at the club that was just up the street. It was The Haig. It was where I saw the Red Norvo Trio with Tal Farlow, guitar and Red Mitchell, bass. And, of course where I heard the genius Art Tatum for the first time (or was it Errol Garner). I don't remember because I also saw Art Tatum at a club on 3rd Street in downtown Los Angeles.

The Haig became our hangout, and in a very short time, when TIME Magazine and others wrote about the pianoless quartet, the place was packed. There were lines around the corner. Our being there particularly every night at the beginning made us like part of the family. The bartender, Jimmy, didn't care if we were old enough to drink because he didn't use liquor anyway. And when he did, he just floated a few drops on the top of the drink. Not because we were underage, but because everyone's drinks were made the same way. The bar had empty bottles on the back bar. When they sold a few drinks they would send someone out to buy a pint of liquor, bourbon or scotch, depending on what was selling that night.

There was a waitress there named Winnie who was a true comedienne with whom we became very friendly. Winnie and her husband Ben remained friends with us for years, going to each other's house when my parents came. My mother would cook for them and Winnie and Ben would make a New York style cheesecake second to none and bring it over to the house. My father loved it more than anyone. Every so often at the club, Winnie would come by and set drinks on the table and say, "These are on that sport over there," pointing to just anyone in the room. The club had gotten so hot and the lines were getting longer and longer. If we were in line and a table emptied, Winnie would come to the door and say, "Gene and his party, please come in." And we would go in. A couple of times people complained and Winnie would yell, "They had reservations, Sport!" Once, when some guy left a dime tip, which was change on his bill, Winnie yelled, "Hey, Sport. Come back and get your dime, you need it more than I do." He ran out like a wet cat.

Any big name act that played the Coconut Grove across the street from The Haig, would invariably come to The Haig. No one paid attention to them. The jazz was so good that's all you wanted to hear and see. The original group had Gerry, Chet Baker on trumpet, Bob Whitlock on bass and Chico Hamilton on drums. Chet had a tone that was unforgettable, and he and Gerry were so good together. Bob Whitlock laid down a solid bass line and Chico was remarkable to watch. He used hands, fingers, elbows, brushes, and he hummed like another musical instrument. In time, Carson Smith replaced Bob Whitlock on bass. But Chico was still a one-man orchestra.

One night as we were standing in line to get into the Haig, Harry Belafonte was leaving the club (he was working at the Coconut Grove). I yelled out, "Hi, Harry" and he waved back and said, "Hi, how you doing?" He left and just after that Winnie called out, "Gene and his party, come in, please." She sat us at Belafonte's table and told us, "I got rid of him to seat you guys." She was kidding of course. My sister asked me, "How do you know Belafonte?" I told her, "The same way you do, from records and pictures." Vasso, who had come in from San Bernardino, and Kiki both stood there with their mouths open. Belafonte did that to women, he was so handsome. He had done a couple of records that I liked, *Close Your Eyes*, among others and a song he brought back from Japan with a lovely melody called *Gomenasai*. We all thought it would become a big hit but it didn't. But we did see him at

The Haig many times and he always said hi to us. After a couple of times he probably thought he knew us well. Needless to say, he was probably one of the few artists who could use only one name – Belafonte. He stood with Martin Luther King and his stance on the United States foreign policy of today is like a breath of fresh air.

Chapter 15

Vasso had not come into Los Angeles for a few weeks and the night that she did come in Chico Hamilton did not remember her. He said hi to all of us by name. He didn't say anything to Vasso at all. The DOWNBEAT Reader's Poll had come out that week and Chico did not come in within the top five choices so Vasso said, "I'm glad he didn't win the DOWNBEAT Poll. Imagine, he forgot me already." Of course, it was a joke but that night we told about it and we all laughed. Those few months of great joy and happiness would later turn to sadness. We had become accustomed to being in The Haig three or four nights a week, like a family.

A short time after that, Gerry announced that Chico was leaving to go on tour with Lena Horne. We cried. We were telling him not to go because the group wouldn't sound the same. This group was so great. He explained why he had to go (it would further his career). And he loved Lena Horne. We gave him leave to go but we made him promise to come back. Larry Bunker came and fell right in. We liked him a lot too. But, man, did we dig Chico and how we missed him. I remember when they were discussing whom to bring in when Chico left. One of the waitresses said, "Stan Levey" and Winnie yelled out, "Stan Levey? He'll blow the (expletive) roof off this damn place. He'd be great at the Hollywood Palladium. This place is a closet."

A final scene. The Haig was swinging. Packed audiences nightly and everyone groovy and respectful. Some nights the group played moody subtle tunes and you were grateful for those audiences who listened. But sometimes trouble comes from where you don't expect it.

This particular night one of the owners of The Haig came in and sat at the bar. He was always loud trying to impress his current girlfriend. Gerry and Chetty were playing a ballad *Moonlight in Vermont* and the counterpoint was spine tingling. Chico was using his mallets and then his fingers on the drums. It was one of those glorious moments that happen in jazz when people appreciate the music, and the musicians know it and they blow. Just at that time we heard laughter, which was quite loud and getting louder. People in the club began saying, "Shhh… shhh." The laughing stopped and sure enough it was the owner. In seconds, it started again and this time it was really offensive. The music stopped abruptly and you could hear a pin drop. No sound at all. Gerry looked at the bar where the owner was seated, stared at him for a long moment and then said, "You're a noisy cat, aren't you?" The band left the stand, went back into the dressing room, got their stuff and left. I don't remember how many days passed before the group returned, but I was so proud of Gerry. He never lost his cool.

Too many people think jazz doesn't need to be listened to. They think its background music. Jazz is no less important than any classical piece of music. I can still hear Gerry and Chetty playing counterpoint that even Bach himself would dig. The baritone sax, despite its size, in Gerry's hands could also become as soft and as melodic as any other musical instrument.

One Sunday at the Lighthouse in Hermosa Beach, we got there early because we heard that various jazz artists were coming to sit in with the regular group, which consisted that day of Shelly Manne, Bob Cooper, Bud Shank and the owner and bass player Howard Rumsey among others. Miles Davis was also supposed to come. We wanted some sun and swimming because surely, if Miles was there we would never want to leave. The joy of the Lighthouse was that you could go swimming and then just sit in the club with a drink and dig great jazz. We got there just before noon and swam for about an hour and then went into the club and got a drink.

We sat at the bar since they were still setting up the tables. We looked around to ask someone when the music was going to start. That's when we heard an argument and the bartender was yelling at someone. We looked and it was Miles Davis, and that's when we first saw him. Miles yelled back from the other end of the rounded bar. The bartender called Miles a "fucking nigger" and we were shocked because we had never heard that at home and certainly not in the places we frequented. There were mixed jazz groups and patrons everywhere and there was no problem in New Hampshire or Massachusetts. The bartender was a big hulking guy who was coming over the bar to fight with Miles.

My brother, Steve, all five foot nine of him, grabbed the bartender's arm as he was coming over the bar. He then pulled the bartender down onto the bar and held him there. We used to call Steve the "barbarian" because when he got mad he could bring down King Kong. He had fought in the Navy having beaten some Golden Glove champs and would have become a professional except that my parents did not want him to do so. They felt that fighting was too barbaric and cited the original Olympic Games as proof. The Greeks outlawed boxing when a fighter got hit in the mouth and swallowed his own teeth. But later, Rome adopted it.

While the fighting was going on inside, someone went outside and called in a cop. Two cops who were on duty on the street in front of the Lighthouse came in. They immediately approached Miles and asked him what the trouble was. Before he could answer, the other bartender or just another employee of the club jumped into the conversation and blamed my brother and Miles for starting the fight. I jumped up with righteous indignation and told them I was a witness and that I would be willing to go to court to explain what had happened. One of the cops asked me to tell him what happened. So, in my most mellifluous tones I told him that the fight was started when the bartender called Miles Davis a "fucking nigger." The cop said, "Oh, so you know him?" I said, "I know who he is but I don't know him personally. He is one of the country's greatest musicians." The cop told me to continue with my story. "Officer," I said, "when the bartender called him 'nigger' they argued and the bartender started to come over the bar. This gentleman here," pointing to my brother, "stepped in to stop the fight. That's really all that happened."

Silence for a long moment. "Okay, just forget it and go about your business," said the cop. And that was the end of it. We got to talk to Miles for a long time. That was a big thrill for all of us. We tried to show him how much we loved him and his music and that not everyone is prejudiced. It was an embarrassing incident for all of us. Later, Miles did appear on the bandstand and played beautifully. Bob Cooper got up after that and played *My One and Only Love* on oboe. It might have been another day, but somehow I remember that the highlights of that day were two of beauty and one very ugly. God save us from the latter!

We spoke to Miles again later in the evening. That was always a gas. Following Miles' career through his recording output is a way of experiencing the evolution in his music. *Miles Ahead*, *Milestones*, *Porgy and Bess*, *Kind of Blue* and *Sketches of Spain* are among my favorites. There are many others, among which you'll find your own personal favorites. On the whole, his total output is extremely valuable, enticing, and thoroughly enjoyable.

Miles naturally influenced many musicians. Chet Baker, who Gerry Mulligan (in jest) called Chesney, was a Miles admirer but he also had a tone that was all his own. He was a quiet, shy and soft-spoken young man. After opening at The Haig, we saw him practically every night. Chetty would come in and say "Hi" and then go over and sit in a corner until it was time to play. We used to go there early because we stayed for only the first set during the week since we all worked. Although many times, everybody was so "on" that we stayed until 2 A.M. Thankfully, we were a block away from home and able to get five or six hours sleep (I couldn't do that today). We would talk to Winnie and the bartender and laugh it up with their stories about The Haig. When Chetty came in we would invite him over or I would go over and talk to him. Rather, I questioned him about where he was from and who his favorites in music were. When I was one-on-one, he was cool. Otherwise, he was very shy.

One night, Kiki and I went in alone and he came over to our table when we insisted that he sit with us. He explained that he didn't want to butt in when two people were alone. I told him that Kiki was my sister and that all the other people who came in were friends except for Steve who was our brother. Chetty sat and talked and we wanted to buy him a drink. He didn't drink, not even a Coke. Winnie brought him a glass of water because she knew. When Chetty got up to play, Winnie came over and said, "I'm glad he's not a customer. I'd never make a living on him." Winnie would say all kinds of outrageous things that were meant to be funny and they were.

When the first set was over, Chetty came back to our table. He excused himself and took me aside to ask me if he could date Kiki. He was a few years older than I so I found it cool that he would be so formal. I told him to ask her because it was her decision. Well, Kiki never did date him because she was afraid. And we all remained friends…friends of the club, friends of Winnie and Ben and everyone else at The Haig. That night, when Chetty asked me if he could date Kiki, was also the night that I found out how much he loved Billie Holiday. Since he was planning to do an album of singing he would try to do a couple of Billie's songs. I told him that I thought that was great because I loved Billie and because it was she who introduced me to jazz. He loved Lady's phrasing and sense of time but most of all he loved that she never yelled or screamed. He really was moved by the fact that she got her emotions across without screaming.

Chapter 16

When the group resurrected *My Funny Valentine,* it became as big a hit as a jazz record could get. It was requested every night and in both sets. One very hot summer night, we did not go into the club because The Haig had no air conditioning. As fate would have it, when we passed the front door we heard the trumpet start playing *My Funny Valentine.* It was a quiet night and Chetty's beautiful tone just floated out of the back window. We had to stop to listen. The window was at the far end of the bar and Jim kept it open when it was hot. Chetty's tone was so lyrical and though we had heard him play it dozens of times, this time it was very, very cool. We could not move. I know some of you will think that's very dramatic, but it is a fact.

It happened again a few years later when I went to see another favorite jazz singer, Anita O'Day. It was a very intimate club off the corner of Crescent Heights Boulevard and Sunset Boulevard on the Sunset Strip. I was managing an Israeli restaurant and nightclub and I closed early that night – just so I could catch Anita's last set. As I walked into the club, I heard the intro to *Lush Life* being played on the piano. By the time I reached the actual room, she had started singing the verse. I stood at the door leaning against the doorjamb and I literally could not move. Her version was so true to the song that the only other version I loved as much was Nat King Cole's, which is a classic. Anita's version was as if she had lived it and in part she did.

This is just one of the musical pieces written by Billy Strayhorn, who also wrote *Take the A Train* for the band of Duke Ellington which became the band's theme song. He was with Ellington from the late

Thirties until his death in May of 1967. Billy Strayhorn wrote songs and arrangements and played piano and all of it was unique and beautiful. I said earlier that this period of about one year in my life is a unique high point because I had learned so much. There were to be other times, but the search for records, hearing great music and meeting good people were rare in such a short period of time. It will never happen again. You do, of course, think of the good times. When Chetty started singing, I couldn't get over how he sang like he played his trumpet because by this time we had gotten to know his style. Ah, but every so often you would hear the slurs or the elongated tones of Billie. No, he didn't copy her. Rather, she influenced him. So much so that he did a tribute album called *Baker's Holiday.* He presented a true tribute to her.

His vocal of *My Funny Valentine* also became a hit and they tried to make him a teen idol. Thankfully it didn't work. He became a favorite of mine, not because I knew him but because he sounded so good. Many people did not like his voice, but hearing his vocal albums made here and in Italy you feel the warmth and the intimacy and the long flowing lines of melody. In Italy in 1962, he recorded an instrumental version of *Over the Rainbow* that has both the pain and the lost hope that obviously was his at that time. The pictures that I saw of him, taken during the last period of his life, depressed me for a long, long time. I remembered the Chet Baker that I knew who loved music so much that it was the most important part of his life.

A documentary film called *Let's Get Lost* has him singing and playing, and it gets increasingly sad as you see the life of someone you know go down the road to destruction. There has been talk in the past about making a film of his life, which was coupled with the idea that he was another tragic James Dean. Now that a new biography of Chet Baker's life has been published, that talk is here again. Hollywood, with very rare exceptions, has destroyed the life of practically everyone depicted on film. Let these people rest in peace. I don't say this because I am like many others who condemn Hollywood simply because it exists. I work in Hollywood.

This might be the time to thank Clint Eastwood for his movie on Charlie Parker, *Bird.* There was only one thing wrong with it – it wasn't long enough. I didn't want it to end! Now if Clint Eastwood were interested in doing Chet Baker's life, I would say "great." Eastwood has the knowledge and the ability to make a film interesting, no matter what the subject. A quick look at the variety of films he has been associated with would be ample proof of his greatness. But to let anyone else do it would be a disaster. No, let Chet rest in peace. Jazz movies as a rule do not make much money anyway and most times the stories are bastardized beyond recognition, as I said before. So why do it, unless you do it honestly without sensationalizing it. Just dig his records; it should more than suffice.

Art Pepper would come by to see Gerry and if Gerry wasn't there, he felt very comfortable about coming upstairs and hanging with us until Gerry came home. That's the kind of relationship we had with most of the musicians. We could discuss anything under the sun, not only jazz. What a great player he was. What amazed me most about him as a human being was his emotional sensitivity. I should have known what kind of a man he was because of his playing. We always had a lot of fun with him. But one night, he came to the apartment and he was miserable. He had separated from his wife. He told us how much he loved her and how he felt about her. It was so moving I can't forget his hands as he spoke. It was like he was fingering his sax but he was really holding his wife. I saw him many times in clubs when he came to town. And we always went to see him. He was influenced by Charlie Parker as so many others were. He found his own voice and he blossomed into the higher ranks of modern jazz. As a true disciple of Bird's, his recordings are still wondrous.

Chapter 17

Producer Norman Granz brought his "Jazz at the Philharmonic" back to Los Angeles yearly. He had started the show in Los Angeles sometime in 1944. He gave jazz artists the chance to have a jam session and to play what they wanted to play. This time around, Lester Young was with the group along with some of the regular stars of "Jazz at The Philharmonic". And again, we were still not solvent. How could we get in? Through the musicians, we had met many people, most of whom were jazz fans. Lois was our friend and girlfriend of one of these musicians.

She claimed that she knew Irving Granz, Norman Granz's brother; she said she could get us in for free. So, the three of us went with her. She had a southern accent. She was drop-dead gorgeous…five feet eight inches of woman. What she had for a brain is questionable. At the door of the auditorium, she demanded of the guard standing there that it was imperative that she see Irving Granz. They told her he wasn't there but she was firm. She started running around like a crazy roadrunner from the box office to the main door, to the backstage door and again to the front. She was all over the place and attracting people's attention. I was ready to give up, but I would not leave because I had to see Lester young (Pres). I could bear all the embarrassment that Lois had inflicted on us. But deep down, I was saying, "Go get 'em, baby." Pres had never come to Los Angeles during my initial time there. At no time was he in New York when I was there. I stood there praying and my prayers were answered. I don't know how Lois did it! She called us and we joined one of the security guards who opened doors and talked to people and what else I can't remember. Before I knew it, we were backstage with all the musicians talking and tuning and my adrenaline was high!

Sure enough, she knew Irving Granz or she convinced the guy at the door because he told us to go backstage and said that Irving was there. This was my first backstage adventure. We went backstage and passed the stars of "Jazz at The Philharmonic" like Dizzy Gillespie and Ella Fitzgerald and bumped right into Pres. He was taller than I expected, and I saw his loafers and his unique clothes. He had even created his own language so to speak and in time others caught on. He was wearing his pork pie hat as usual. He was the Pres and there he was standing in front of me. I was in awe of his charisma. He was one of the most truly original human beings ever. I thought of his music, especially from Billie's recordings like *Easy Living*, *Sailboat in the Moonlight*, *All of Me*, and *Me, Myself, and I*. I couldn't talk. I loved his music so much but Lois broke the spell. She practically pulled his sax case out of his hand to carry it for him. Pres coolly and gently took it back. We talked at length, but he seemed to be a little withdrawn. When I told him which of his recordings I liked, he saw that I knew his work well, so he opened up a little and told me his favorites of his own recordings. It was another one of those great moments of my life. Again, it was too brief.

After about thirty minutes, we were told to leave the backstage area. We left and went out front as the concert was about to begin. We had no seats so we moved into some empty ones. As the people who had tickets for those seats arrived, we moved into other empty seats. We did this three or four times, and in the end we ended up standing in the back. The place was sold out.

Pres was not a disappointment, especially with *These Foolish Things* and *Lester Leaps In*. The applause was not excessive. I thought it should have been. There was another tenor player, a very good one, who on this particular night started the honking which had become a fad. He was on his back rolling on the floor and the people were screaming, yelling for more. I was very angry that night. How could they not feel the superiority of Pres' playing? My greatest consolation was that I had at least heard him play in person and that was enough.

Pres was in the Army and had a terrible time of it primarily due to the racism of one of his superiors. He was originally sent to Georgia and he said that that alone could make him blow his top. When he got out of the Army all his disciples were making money and he had trouble getting a job. As they had done with Billie, there was talk that he was through and not the same Pres as the one who went into the Army. I guess these people who think that way never change. They just stay the same. One need only read what he went through in the Army to know that he was not the same. In time, he created many beautiful records and they are there for all to hear. He was still the master. The saddest picture I have ever seen was one of Pres sitting on the edge of a bed in a hotel room with his sax in his lap. The caption under the picture read, "NO ONE SAID THANKS." Thankfully and finally, there is now a biography on the life of this genius. It is essential that anyone interested in jazz should at least read it if not own it.

Chapter 18

We met the drummer Shelly Manne, at the Lighthouse and he was a gas! He liked "halva". We would take him some and he would call it "halava." I told him he had to say it the Greek way or he wouldn't get it. He never did. It was always "halava" to him.

Musicians who came from New York would visit the Lighthouse and sit in with the house band. Musicians there at various times were Max Roach, Bob Cooper, Bud Shank, Jimmy Giuffre, Buddy Collette, and Sonny Clark. Other great musicians who appeared there were Hampton Hawes, Laurindo Almeda, Sonny Criss, Clare Fischer, Gerald Wilson, Cal Tjader, Sonny Rollins, Cannonball Adderley, Bill Perkins, Warne Marsh, and many others who were recorded at the Lighthouse in the 50s and 60s. It was a great time for jazz. Both coasts were swinging and influencing each other. Musicians became more bi-coastal than ever.

We didn't have a car, so we depended on friends who had cars to take us to the Lighthouse or Central Avenue. Luckily, we could walk to The Haig or the Tiffany Club or we would take a short bus ride downtown to see the likes of Duke Ellington and the Nat King Cole Trio at the Paramount Theater. We also took the red car to go to Hollywood Boulevard to see Jack and Charlie Teagarden or Dave Brubeck and Paul Desmond.

One night we decided to go to bed early, and at about midnight, when I was still awake, I heard Kiki's voice say, "Who's at the Tiffany Club?"

I said, "Stan Getz."

"Who else?" she asked.

"Anita O'Day," I answered.

She said, "Let's go!"

We got up, got dressed and walked to the Tiffany Club a few blocks away. When we walked in, we saw Stan Getz over at a corner table. We walked over to him and said hello. He thanked us for coming. During this period of time, Getz was on a health kick and he had gained a lot of weight. Because of this, I said, "Stanley, have you had your milk today?" We all broke up laughing because that's what Gerry would ask Getz whenever he would come to the house. His set was just fantastic and his playing was better than ever. And what can one say about Anita O'Day? Except that she was always improvising and swinging. On another occasion, Anita had told me that she idolized Billie Holiday all her life and she finally met her backstage at one of the jazz festivals. When they were introduced, Anita was thrilled and Billie nonchalantly said hi and kept on walking. Anita stood there all alone and said as if to herself, "That's my idol!" And then she said to me, "And she will always be my idol no matter what."

Another time, a group of us went to the Tiffany Club to see Slim Gaillard who sang and played piano. Chris Connor was the other half of the bill. We sat at the half-moon piano bar, which was right in front of the bandstand. We had never seen Slim Gaillard before, but we knew of the many songs he had written, like *Cement Mixer* and *Yapra Harisi*. The latter was a series of names of several different Armenian and Arabic foods. My Armenian friend, Joe explained the meaning, but I can't remember what the names all meant except that one of them meant stuffed grape leaves. The music to all of these tunes usually was really good swinging jazz. He wrote many songs, which were of that ilk, like his biggest hit *Flat Foot Floogie*, which I used to sing as a kid.

My brother, Steve asked me something in Greek and Slim answered for me in perfect Greek. We all laughed and continued speaking Greek to each other. We then asked him where he learned all his Greek and he told us that his father had taken him to Greece where they spent a few years.

Chris Connor, who was from the Anita O'Day school of singers, had recently left Stan Kenton to become a soloist and this was her first L.A. gig. She did a terrific set and we knew we would hear from her again, especially after her rendition of Kurt Weill's *My Ship*.

After Chris' set, Slim came and sat with us. We had a great time, which is when he told us that jazz drummer, Johnny Otis was Greek. Otis also fronted an R&B band and played throughout the L.A. area. For all practical purposes, he had embraced the black musical culture to the extent that everyone thought he was black. We went to see him one night when he was playing at a club on the south side of L.A. We spoke to him in Greek but very little knowledge of Greek had remained. That was fine because his music swung and we danced like crazy that night. I was very proud that a Greek was involved in jazz and R&B. I also asked him about the legendary Leo Watson who had played with Slim. I had read how unique a singer he was. It was at times like this that I felt that I was born about ten years too late. I finally heard Leo Watson on an LP produced by Leonard Feather. I thought Watson was really the innovator of this kind of scat singing.

When Art Pepper told us that he was playing with Stan Kenton at the Valley Ballroom in San Bernardino, we all hopped into a car and went. What a night! In the sax section, was Ritchie Kamuka on tenor sax whom we had met at the Lighthouse. His idol was Lester Young, so naturally we loved him. Art Pepper, of course, was playing alto sax, as was a new member whose name was Lennie Niehaus. Art told us we should really listen to him because he was a great addition to the band. The drummer was Shelley Manne who had introduced a song at the Lighthouse called *Blues in Burlesque ("I'd rather drink muddy water than sleep in a hollow log")*. He performed it that night and again he brought down the house--it was a showstopper. Years later, I saw Lennie Niehaus' name in the credits of Clint Eastwood's film *Bird* and continued to see it in many other Eastwood films. It was great to see jazz musicians expand into other mediums. A few months later at the Valley Ballroom, we saw the great Lionel Hampton Band. This was the last big band that we saw since this was the end of the big band era. Now we had bop and the cool sounds of the West Coast jazz.

Hampton Hawes was one of my favorite pianists on the West Coast. He played at most of the local jazz clubs and so we saw him on a regular basis. Unfortunately, he died too young. Like so many great jazz players, it always was sad when you heard about a death. But when we heard that Clifford Brown died in a car accident at the age of twenty-five, we were shattered. What a talent! I knew him from his recordings with

Max Roach. Through Brownie, as he was called, I discovered Quincy Jones and Helen Merrill on one of her greatest albums. I loved Brownie's sound and whenever I saw his name on an LP I bought it. As for Quincy Jones, I never saw him, but I knew his work from the time that he was playing trumpet in Dizzy Gillespie's big band. He was twenty-three. He has written for Count Basie, Sarah Vaughn, Billy Eckstine, Dinah Washington and Frank Sinatra. It is a personal pleasure for me when a man of this caliber influences other forms of music with his jazz sounds.

Annie Ross, who was singing around town in the jazz scene, wrote lyrics to two of Wardel Grey's recordings. One was *Jackie* and the other was *Twisted* which caused quite a stir in jazz circles. It received far greater success when Annie teamed up with two innovators of jazz vocalese: Jon Hendricks and Dave Lambert. Hendricks wrote some profoundly hip lyrics that were truly a jazz language for everyone. They did a salute to Count Basie called, "Sing a Song of Basie" and a couple of other albums using the musical gems of Charlie Parker on alto, Miles Davis on trumpet, and Sonny Rollins on tenor sax, among others. Then they did "Sing Along with Basie" with Basie's band and singer Joe Williams. They landed on the cover of TIME Magazine and were called the "Hottest New Group in Jazz", and the "James Joyces of Jazz" and indeed they were! Pick up any one of their albums and you'll think it was recorded yesterday. The occurrence of a jazz group being on the cover of TIME is indeed very rare. Very few jazz musicians have achieved this. Annie went on to do a solo album with Gerry Mulligan, which is a complete and utter joy. She also did an album with tenor saxman Zoot Sims, and that too was first class.

Chapter 19

One night after work, I went to my cousin, Steve's bar. When I came in, he went to the mike and put in a quarter. He told the girl that I was there. She said, "Gene, here's a present from me to you." The record started playing and it was a blues and Lady Day was singing it. A new record. I had never heard it. It was *Rocky Mountain Blues* and I loved it. I put in a quarter and told her to play the other side. It was called *Blue Turning Gray Over You*. In time, I found out that she had recorded two records on the Aladdin label. The other one had *Detour Ahead* and *Be Fair to Me*.

Since these four Aladdin sides, there was nothing new from Billie. Only the last few sides recorded for Decca. Then DOWNBEAT started advertising a new release for Norman Granz, which we had heard about at the Tiffany Club earlier that year. He had been recording his "Jazz At The Philharmonic" series in addition to the major jazz greats. There was no one better than Norman Granz for Billie to record with because he was a true lover of jazz. It was a ten-inch LP with eight songs backed by a small group consisting of Flip Phillips on tenor sax, Charlie Shavers on trumpet, Alvin Stoller on drums, Ray Brown on bass, and Oscar Peterson on piano. This was particularly exciting for me because reviews were coming from the East Coast that Billie was in great shape and breaking records at various clubs, but not in New York. She could not perform in any club where alcohol was being sold.

I had found a record store on the corner of Fifth and Los Angeles Street in a hotel in Los Angeles. The Clef sides for Norman Granz were not out except for a 78 of *Lover Come Back to Me* and *Yesterdays*, which I bought and which were both chosen as Records of the Year by METRONOME Magazine. A couple of years earlier, METRONOME Magazine chose *Porgy* as Record of the Year. It was the same year that DOWNBEAT gave it a two-star rating with the comment: "...a great singing style has lapsed into over ornate sloppiness." *Porgy* and the flip side *My Man* can in no stretch of the imagination be called "sloppy".

METRONOME kept their critics mostly intact for years. They were the first to support bop when most people ridiculed it. Billie had lost her cabaret license to work in New York. She did concerts and radio shows, but as stated earlier, she could not work where liquor was sold. Few in New York knew of her work at that time, unless you went to a concert where she was performing or sought out her records. So they all jumped on the bandwagon that Billie was in a decline. She came back from some club dates in Boston, Sacramento, Chicago, Los Angeles, in addition to a gig at Carnegie Hall and the reviews from these cities were uniformly excellent. Carnegie Hall was a huge success, and the radio broadcasts from the Storyville Club in Boston were marvelous sides that were released after her death. Stan Getz backs her on three sides and she also does a version of *Porgy* that is in a class by itself. From Boston, Nat Hentoff sent glowing reports, which were printed in the jazz magazines. Unfortunately, in New York, certain critics had not heard her on these radio broadcasts and were unable to assess her then current performances. The critics who saw her in clubs around the country attested to her still great performances.

There was a TV show in Los Angeles hosted by Peter Potter and various artists who would bring in a record that they thought should be a hit. A singer, named Frances Faye, brought in *Crazy He Calls Me* and *You're My Thrill*. She spoke glowingly about Billie's new record on Decca. Needless to say, it didn't win. The next time Frances Faye was in town, I went to see her. There were two clubs on the Sunset Strip that featured jazz. Gene Norman's Crescendo on the street level and upstairs was a club called The Interlude. I don't know if Gene Norman owned both of them, although I think he did. But no matter, both clubs really swung. At various times, we saw Count Basie, Lionel Hampton, Mel Torme, The Mary Kaye Trio, and of course, Frances Faye. She was not really a jazz singer, but she was jazz influenced and had a couple of LPs released on the Bethlehem label with jazz greats backing her. She and

Mel Torme whom I have long admired, did a three-LP jazz version set of *Porgy and Bess* with The Russ Garcia and Duke Ellington orchestras. There was Frank Rosolino on trombone, Howard McGhee on trumpet, singers Johnny Hartmann and Betty Roche, and on drums, my buddy Chico Hamilton among other jazz greats. So when you went to see Frances Faye, she swung. She was musical and funny, and with bongo player, Jack Constanzo, they rocked the house. It was through this recording that I discovered a singer named Bev Kelly who was with the Pat Moran Quartet on the *Porgy and Bess* LP. She is another great jazz singer, but there are only two LPs by her. I don't know anything about her except that she is in that long, long line of Billie Holiday-influenced singers and she can really sing. Of course, the drummer on the Porgy set was Chico Hamilton. That's how jazz is. One artist leads you to another and that in turn makes you a jazz fan for life.

Billie – Jazz City, L.A. Circa 1956

Billie with Gene – High Hat Club, Boston – 1950-1951

Billie – Jazz City, L.A. Circa 1956

Billie with Louis McKay (Husband) Circa 1956

Billie with Gene – Jazz City, L.A. Circa 1956

Billie – Date unknown

Billie – San Francisco 1950's

Billie – San Francisco 1950's

Billie – San Francisco 1950's

Billie – San Francisco 1950's

Billie – San Francisco 1950's

Billie – Europe 1954

Billie – Europe 1954 (L to R – Red Mitchell, Billie,
Buddy defranco, Red Norvo)

Front of Christmas Card to Gene from Gerry Mulligan and Group

Inside of card to Gene from Gerry Mulligan and Group

Chapter 20

I was working in a Greek restaurant a few years ago and we catered to many celebrities. A Hollywood beauty of the 50s and 60s was having a birthday party at her Bel Air home. I went when I found out that Mel Torme was going to sing at the party. I did all the organizational obligations that my duties called for and then I went around looking for Torme. In time, I found him alone on the patio overlooking the mountains and I cornered him for one of the most pleasing talks I ever had with anyone. We discussed his records and when he asked me which one was my favorite, I told him and he flipped. He said, "All my friends loved that album." He couldn't explain why but I said that for me it was his best because I felt he had reached the deepest understanding in his lyrics that I had ever heard from him. An added plus, was the alto player, Phil Woods who was on the recording date with strings arranged by the orchestra leader, Chris Gunning. In the final analysis, as in the life of most jazz artists, whatever success they have—they are still underrated in comparison to the musicians today who sell clothes, hairstyles and "image." That night at the party he sang *Lulu's Back In Town* and *Our Love is Here to Stay* so effortlessly. It was another truly groovy jazz night.

Billie Holiday's initial LP on Clef Records was a ten-inch LP with eight songs as was the second eight-song LP. Both received five stars in DOWNBEAT as well as a B+ rating from METRONOME for the second LP. Billie was on track and these new releases were the continuation of an evolving jazz artist.

While at the apartment on Kenmore, we had houseguests practically every weekend. Some friends from my high school class were in the service and they all came to visit. We showed them Los Angeles and it was good to be with old friends in a new environment. In the summer, we would take the bus at the corner of Wilshire and Kenmore and go straight down to Santa Monica. The beach was clean then and the people were few. Santa Monica held a special place in my heart because of Humphrey Bogart films. It is because of one of those films that I am still a Scotch drinker. My brother Yanni would also come home on his leave from the Marines and it was like a reunion. On my 18th birthday, my sister, who is a great cook but a better baker, baked a birthday cake and invited Gerry and Carol to come up to have dinner and celebrate my birthday. I acted blasé and said, "I'm not a baby to have a birthday party," and Gerry said very softly, "You should just say 'Thank you', that your sister is so nice in giving you a birthday party". So very obsequiously I said, "Thank you," and we all laughed and enjoyed the party. We always talked about music, jazz in particular, but now we had reached the point where we were discussing a plethora of subjects. Of course, we also had a lot of laughs with Carol, who was a very funny character. She was almost as funny as Winnie and she also had that southern accent, which lent itself to her kind of humor while Winnie was a 100% New Yorker.

When my parents came, we had rented a large three-bedroom house and bought furniture for all six rooms. Thankfully, I was still working at the discount house and they gave me great advice and credit. We picked up the folks at Union Station with a thousand images of trains coming and going from the films I had seen. (Trains still thrill me!) When we got home they walked into the house and they both started crying. We all cried tears of joy. We always maintained that we had the best parents of anyone we knew. My father looked at my mother and said, "I told you we had good children." That was the second time in my life that I saw my father cry.

Chapter 21

The first and only other time I saw my father cry was when we got a letter from Greece telling us that our grandfather, his father, had died of starvation at the age of seventy-two during WWII. The Nazis had taken their sheep, goats, pigs, ducks, rabbits, olives, olive oil, and their wine. There was nothing left to eat except the wild greens that grew everywhere. Primarily, they ate endives and dandelion greens but without olive oil. So they were obliged to use only lemon juice. There was a saying in Greece at the time that the reason more people didn't die is because the Nazis could not take the fruit bearing trees and the greens with them. Still, they devastated Greece. The resistance in Greece never ceased during the years of occupation. As a result, the Nazis killed all the males in some villages and completely wiped out many others. All of this was done by the Nazis as reprisal for the sabotage against the occupation forces by the Greek guerillas. It is no wonder then that one out of every nine Greek citizens was killed during this horrific occupation.

Having become acclimated to his new surroundings in Los Angeles, my father continued his constant curiosity for any and all things. In time, he discovered the Grand Central Market in downtown Los Angeles. Every Saturday, he would take a bus downtown and would bring us Genoa salami, Polish kielbasa, Danish boiled ham, French Brie, etc. As for the Greek products, there was a market across the street from the Greek Church. On Sundays, we bought Feta cheese, olives, and Greek sesame bread rings, among other things. Since we didn't eat breakfast before going to church, by the time we got home, we had already eaten two of the three sesame bread rings we had bought. This necessitated buying four rings of bread so we could have enough to take some home. My parents and some new found friends would go to the beach for fresh fish and pick wild endives and dandelion greens to go with the fish. For them it was like returning to their childhood in Greece. We were settling into a new and happy life in Southern California.

One fine day, I received a letter telling me that I was to report for active duty in the U.S. Army. The day I was to report was the 9th of July. That was two years to the day that I left New Hampshire to come to Los Angeles. What a tremendous two years that was! I hoped that every two-year period would be as good. So now it was the Army for two years with eighteen months of that in Nuremberg, Germany. After taking a test, I got a Military Occupation (M.O.) as a Greek Interpreter. They told me that the Army would send me to Greece as an interpreter, but only if I signed up for another year. I would have to spend six months at the Presidio of Monterrey to perfect my Greek. I didn't want to do that. So they sent me to Germany with the proviso that if they needed me, it would not take too long for get me to Greece. I'm sorry that I didn't stay in for another year. Because after I had taken two trips to Greece, while in the Army, I fell in love with the country and the people.

So, I finally got to Bremerhaven, Germany. We boarded a train for Nuremberg where I was to be stationed. It was mid-December and it was cold. At 10 PM, we arrived at Nuremberg. We were picked up and taken to the casern (barracks). Even though the mess hall was closed, they fed us. There was no war going on so things were really cool. The only reason I went to Europe was because of my M.O. Otherwise, I would have been sent elsewhere. On a huge transport ship, we were sent to Germany. It was a very boring trip except for the dolphins which we encountered in the Mid-Atlantic. For about four or five days, it was an exhilarating experience. The trip lasted eleven days. The sea was rough most of the time and many of the guys got seasick.

We were all assigned to various work details, but we all went to sick call to avoid that. The lines, of course, were staggering. Every day was a new funny scene. The funniest of all concerned a slightly overweight soldier named Winthrop. About the sixth day out, I happened to be behind him in line. There were no private offices for us. One soldier would be talking to the doctor while the next guy stood behind him waiting at the doorway. They moved us out quickly. That day, the conversation went like this,

Doctor: (In amazement) "What! Six days?"

Winthrop: "Yes, sir."

Doctor: "Did you take the pills I gave you?"

Winthrop: "Yes, sir."

Doctor: "And what happened?"

Winthrop: "Nothing, sir."

Doctor: "And you've eaten three meals every day?"

Winthrop: "Yes, sir."

Doctor: "Are you sure?"

Winthrop: "Yes, sir."

Doctor: "Well, son. I don't know what to say. There is nothing else I can do for you. You're either going to shit or pop, one of the two. Report to duty."

Chapter 22

In Nuremberg, we were stationed at the casern where the S.S. troops were quartered. It was more like a fraternity at an Ivy League college. The buildings were all brick. The Nazis really treated these monsters well. Across the quadrangle from where my platoon was stationed was the casern where the Army band was stationed.

One day when the band was returning from a gig, just as they broke ranks, I heard a trumpet, which was reminiscent of Dizzy Gillespie. I flipped! They had marched in with military music and when they were dismissed I heard *Salt Peanuts*. Naturally, I ran to see who it was. It was a tall, black guy who reminded me of Dexter Gordon, the tenor sax player whom I had recently seen at a club in Los Angeles. But this musician's name was Rick Willis and he played trumpet. We immediately became friends.

Rick, like Diz, was also a clown. He had me holding my stomach merely explaining how square the band members were. We talked for a while and he introduced me to two other jazz trumpet players as well as two other members of the band. Since I had just gotten to Nuremberg, I was not allowed a pass for the first thirty days. Within that time, I got to know the musicians well. We would play records and spend time together in the coffee shop. When the time came for me to get a pass, we all went downtown to a German jazz club called the Stork Club. Everybody called me "Greek" and because of that, they were taking me to another club first.

We got to the club and outside was a huge sign saying, "The Fabulous Greek Hillbillies". I rebelled saying, " I'm not going in there!

I want to hear some jazz!" Well, they carried me inside which was a grand entrance to be sure. They planted me in front of the bandstand and said, "Here's another Greek!" But I was in for a pleasant surprise. The hillbilly band was playing American pop music. At the break, I spoke with the members of the band who were all Greek except for one German who played accordion. After all, we were in Germany so we had to hear some "Oom-Pa-Pa". Before we left, they played a couple of Greek songs for me and I told them I'd be back to see them, which I did on many occasions.

Then we went to the Stork Club. That is where the guys would go to jam. They all got up and started playing and I was home. The German musicians were first rate and they really loved jazz. They played all the standards as well as the newer compositions by the jazz artists of the United States, which were mostly in the bop idiom. These were kids who were all in their twenties. The German group played a version of *All the Things You Are* that sounded so good I can still hum it; it was that beautiful. I went back dozens of times. It became my second home.

I became very good friends with the Greek musicians at the Hillbilly. Most of them were brought to Germany as prisoners of war to work in the German factories. When the war was over, many of the Greeks that stayed had married German women and raised families. In fact, the two tailors who worked in our company were also prisoners of war. One of them, who was named Vasili, had a car and we drove to Greece on one occasion for Easter. The other tailor, named Dimitri, could not come with us. When the war was over, Greece became embroiled in a civil war. At that time his neighbor in Greece who wanted Dimitri's land labeled him a communist. I was shocked to hear that but I was told that it was not such a rare thing to happen. As a result, Dimitri was not allowed to return to Greece. He had employed a lawyer and was fighting to be allowed to legally return to Greece. It was really sad because when Vasili and I were leaving, Dimitri said, "Kiss the Greek earth for me and tell the whole country that I am still a Greek and I'll love my country forever whether I ever get to go back or not." I cried that day. Many years later, I heard something that Melina Mercouri said when the junta in Greece confiscated all her property and took away her passport and told her she was not a Greek. Melina Mercouri said, "I was born a Greek and I will die a Greek." In 1821, when Greece rebelled against the Ottoman Turks after four hundred years of enslavement, that was the war cry of the Greek heroes of independence. Melina brought it into the 20th Century just as she had brought the cry for the return of the Greek marbles in the British Museum back to Greece.

Chapter 23

The U.S. Service Club was in a building across the street from the Nuremberg Castle. If I remember correctly, it was the very building where the Nuremberg War Trials were held. My experiences in that building were very different. There was a group of American girls who ran the club for the American servicemen in the area. The U.S. had clubs like this all over Europe. It was like a peacetime version of the USO. There were games, dancing, and shows. It was a good place to meet people from other countries who brought in shows for the G.I.'s entertainment. It was there that Jerry, one of the trumpet players, and I met two girls from England who had come with a very hip show. They were doing things by singers Eddie Jefferson and King Pleasure, along with other bop and vocalese pieces. So Jerry and I took a week's leave and traveled with the group around Germany. Rick was unable to take leave because he was the lead Trumpet. So Carmine Salonia, the 2nd Trumpet, joined us as his replacement. When they left and our week's vacation was over, we went back to soldiering (ahem ahem). Hearing jazz again for seven days straight really broke the routine of Army life. Although I must admit that Army life was not hard at all. It was a five-day job, nine to five, and every night we went into the city.

At the service club, I had met all the staff members. My two favorites were a blond named Kathy who was ditzy and lovable at the same time, and the other one was an Armenian girl from Fresno, California named Georgia. (I knew a lot about the Armenian Genocide and their history because my buddy Joe, he with the yellow DeSoto, was an Armenian.) So we became friends.

We were a group of about eight and had get-togethers as our time dictated. There were two married couples that had their own apartments off the base who were also part of our group. The guys were in the band. We used Carmine & Lee's apartment for socializing and we felt like tourists.

One year, we went to a fashing (Mardi Gras) party. We all went in costume except for Rick who came in street clothes. We had the hardest time trying to get him into some kind of costume. To make a long, long story short, he took a tablecloth off one table, stripped to his shorts, and made a diaper for himself. No, there are no words to tell you what Rick looked like. Imagine, if you can, a six-foot-two-inch handsome black man smiling like the kid who got away with everything in his life simply because he was charming…standing there in a diaper.

The U.S. Service Club as mentioned earlier also brought in acts and groups from the United States. A Greek-American singer named Betty George, who was from my hometown, came with her act to Nuremburg. She had been working with Milton Berle in New York nightspots and had made quite a name for herself. Not a jazz singer, but a world-class beauty. Blue eyes, black hair, porcelain skin, and she could really sing. I spoke to her before she went on, and during her act she sang a Greek love song, which she dedicated to me. It was one of those old songs that my father played on his bouzouki and we would all sing together. As good a time as I was having in Germany, I must admit that I got a little homesick.

On his trip to the various bases around Europe, Rick met a beautiful German girl in Cologne. Before long, he was going to Cologne as often as he could. In time, they were married. It was also at the same time that the sergeant of my platoon, who was also black, asked me to stand up for him when he married his German girlfriend. The groom had a genuine goodness and kindness about him and the bride was a world-class beauty. Her parents had a home in a little village just outside of Nuremberg. It was like a movie set. Multi-colored flowers surrounded the house as if to announce a spring wedding. There was greenery growing up around the house. The church was about five or six buildings away and the groom and I walked up to the church while the bride's family walked towards us. We met at the front door of the church. We went in first, walked up to the altar, and waited for the bride. It was a short ceremony (unlike a Greek wedding) but it was full of love. After the service, we exited and walked around to the back of the church. There were tables set for about fifty people. We laughed, we danced, we ate, and spent a beautiful day together full of happiness and hope. I guess just doing what you believe in is the answer and knowing that you are okay with God.

Finally A Jazz Flash!

Rick had told me that Billie Holiday was coming to Nuremberg and we got tickets to see her. Again there were eight of us in the group and it was good to hear jazz giants again. About a year before leaving, I read an article by Nat Hentoff in a copy of DOWNBEAT which stated that Billie was singing better than ever, that she recently got married, and was singing at Storyville in Boston to rave reviews. This was proven to the audience in Nuremburg. That night she sang *I Cover the Waterfront, Blue Moon, All of Me, I Cried for You, Lover Man, My Man, Detour Ahead, What a Little Moonlight Can Do, Them There Eyes,* and *Billie's Blues* to a standing ovation. They called her back for two encores; the last one was a jam session with Billie wailing at a tempo so fast that the musicians were smiling happily as they played. They were in seventh heaven. Again there was tremendous applause and a standing ovation.

Backing Billie that night was vibist Red Norvo, clarinetist Buddy DeFranco, bassist Red Mitchell, drummer Elaine Leighton, and Billie's pianist Carl Drinkard. With her on the bill were the Red Norvo Trio, the Buddy DeFranco Quartet, and the all-female Beryl Booker Trio. After the show, we tried to go backstage to see her, but it was impossible. She was doing a show every day for about six weeks in various countries. She had to leave right after the show in Nuremburg so she could get to the next city where she was appearing and which was an overnight trip away. In the Army newspaper, there were stories and pictures from Sweden, Norway, Denmark and the other German cities in which Lady had performed. Then she went to France and England and it was all reported in the papers. For me, it was a revelation. I learned how much jazz meant to Europeans. Our newspapers should be like that and report more on jazz. Americans should have embraced jazz long ago. Instead, we want image and celebrity. As for Billie, she probably sang so well because of all the attention she received from the press and the public. She said herself, "In Europe, I'm called an artist."

At the same time, all of Billie's LPs from Norman Grantz on the Clef and Verve labels were getting five star reviews from DOWNBEAT. I was also fortunate in that I could order LPs from the PX. I bought some Ellington, Shorty Rogers, Mulligan and one of my favorite albums until the day I die. I just put it on to listen to it while I write this. (I am back.) Thankfully, I listened to it all and can honestly tell you that there is no way it can be described. It is called *The Quintet-Jazz at Massey Hall* featuring Charlie Parker on alto sax, Dizzy Gillespie on trumpet, Bud Powell on piano, Charlie Mingus on bass, and Max Roach on drums. These geniuses one and all were the people whose music I was listening to while I was growing up and now they were all together on one LP.

Another sweet thing happened that year. I got a Christmas card from Gerry Mulligan saying, "I'll see you in Europe next summer. P.S. Best from us all." The "all" were Red Mitchell on bass, Jon Eardley on trumpet, and Larry Bunker on drums. Jon Eardley was someone I didn't remember meeting before I went into the Army. Obviously, he joined Gerry after I had left for Germany. They all signed the card and the guys in the band thought I was God.

I had shown them the picture I took with Billie at the Hi Hat in Boston. I also received the METRONOME Yearbook with a gorgeous picture of Billie. Jerry from the band cut out the picture from the book and put it on his wall. I had to write home for another copy. METRONOME did write in very glowing terms about Billie's singing at this time and named many of her records as Record of the Year.

In Germany, I would sometimes have to get up early in order to pass out the weapons to the soldiers going out to the field to train. That was my job. The music at that time of the morning was the country music that was so popular at the time. One morning, crazy as it may sound, I heard Billie Holiday. It was from a guest shot that she had sung on radio. I remembered that song; it was called *Maybe You'll Be There*. I jumped out of bed and was knocked out by the song. I called the station and they said it was a record from a radio show but there were no labels on it. I searched for that song for years. Finally, we found out it was done in June 1949 on a radio show called "Just Jazz" in Los Angeles. It's a remarkable record and it took over twenty years to find it! It is on an English label and it was written by pianist Rube Bloom and lyricist Sammy Gallop. I say this because Rube Bloom also wrote (with lyrics by Ted Koehler) another masterpiece by Billie on her last LP called *Don't Worry 'Bout Me.*

Chapter 24

Time passed and soon I was back home in Los Angeles. I enrolled at Los Angeles City College. I took acting and theater arts classes. I also took German since I had learned quite a bit of the language in Germany. I had a full load at night and worked an eight and a half hour day five days a week. On Saturday, I worked for half-a-day until 1pm. When I came home, I would eat and go to sleep. Sometimes I would sleep until Sunday afternoon. Then a date, a party or a movie. On Monday, back to the routine. My bus ride to work was forty minutes and that's when I read and did homework. I did this for a year. An agent saw the final show in which I had the lead and for which I won the best actor award. He wanted me to sign with him. The head of the drama department told me to go to New York and work the boards so I didn't sign with the agent. I left a couple of months later and I went to New York. I audited all the well-known drama classes and some of them twice using a different name and going to a different drama coach within the various studios. Each audit was a learning experience. I started doing things in little theaters and soon I was invited to join a group which did satire, dramatic readings, poetry and plays. It was here that I discovered Garcia Lorca, Dylan Thomas, and increased my knowledge of theatre and literature. The comedy routines we did are still some of the funniest I've ever worked on or seen.

Billie's biography was published. The biography was written with William Dufty and left a lot to be desired because there was so little about some things and nothing about the great musicians who played with her. There was still much more to learn about Billie that was missing. And you can't blame Billie. There were other culprits.

I read the ads in the papers about her concert at Carnegie Hall called "Lady Sings the Blues." The seats were all reserved with the ticket prices being $4. The reviews were tremendous. Pictures in METRONOME had showed trumpeter Buck Clayton kissing Lady's hand as she arrived at Carnegie Hall. I did not have $4 to buy a ticket and even the less expensive seats were sold out. It was one of the saddest moments in my life.

> Nat Hentoff in DOWNBEAT: "... Lady's sound – a texture simultaneously steel–edged and yet soft inside; a voice that was almost unbearably wise in disillusion and yet still childlike, again at the center. The audience was hers from before she sang, greeting her and saying goodbye with heavy long applause. And at one time, the musicians too applauded. It was a night when Billie was on top, undeniably the best and most honest jazz singer alive."

After her autobiography, numerous articles were written about her problems. She still could not get a cabaret card to work in New York. There were also the magazines like METRONOME, DOWNBEAT, HI-FI and MUSIC REVIEW, SATURDAY REVIEW and others, which explored the world of jazz singers, bemoaning the fact that there were very few singers coming up. And in the end it was always Billie who was the yardstick by which to measure all others. There were also many of the critics who continued to ignore her latest recordings or concert performances.

Since the autobiography was bringing generally good reviews and articles about Billie, I wrote to both LOOK Magazine and TIME Magazine asking them to feature Billie on the cover. Following are their responses:

TIME & LIFE BUILDING
ROCKEFELLER CENTER
NEW YORK 20

EDITORIAL OFFICES

October 8, 1956

Dear Mr. Chrono:

  Many thanks for your compliments on the Duke
Ellington cover story (TIME, August 20). Although
we appreciate Billie Holiday's importance in jazz
today, TIME's music editor has not considered it to
be of sufficient national and international importance to warrant a cover story. However, we do
report periodically on Miss Holiday's career and are
enclosing a tearsheet of our latest story on her in
TIME's July 9th issue.

        Cordially yours,

        Marion Sanders

        Marion Sanders
        For the Editors

Mr. Gene Chrono
149 North Edgemont
Los Angeles 4, California

LOOK

COWLES MAGAZINES INC. *Look Building, 488 Madison Ave., New York 22, N. Y., MUrray Hill 8-03*

October 23, 1956

Mr. Gene Chrono
149 No. Edgemont
Los Angeles 4, Calif.

Dear Mr. Chrono:

I am very sorry that I have not been able to answer you
sooner. Several members of our editorial board were away on
extended trips or on vacation when your letter arrived, and
I did want them to see your suggestion that we do an article
about " Billie Holiday. "

Upon their return, our editors gave your letter their
careful consideration, but they regret that they cannot feature
this story in LOOK, since it does not fit their present
editorial needs.

They, nonetheless, are grateful to you for your interest
in LOOK.

Cordially,

Anne Celli

Anne Celli
Assistant to the Editors

AC/sm/mg
Enc.

Chrono was the first theatrical name that I used because I was told in New York that Chronopoulos was too long. Chrono was short but not long on the interviews. During this time, a couple of friends who were in my class at Los Angeles City College came to New York and called me. We ended up living close to each other in the theater district. I discovered the Village Voice and auditioned for many shows, advertised therein, most of which I didn't get. Things were bad. We were all broke. Jim and Tom lived on 53rd and 8th Avenue. I lived at 608 9th Avenue.

I became antsy as to what I should do. I needed a job. A couple of days later, I received a letter telling me to come home for some family matters. Come home with what? I had to get ready saying I'll be home right after New Year's Day. That gave me about six weeks to get solvent. On Thanksgiving Jim, Tom and I had twenty-one cents between us. We found a little market that was open and we bought a can of pork and beans. We now had four cents and asked the grocer to give us a Kaiser roll for four cents. He refused. "It costs five cents," he said. After much ado about a lot, I laid the twenty-one cents on the counter, opened up the bread case and took out a roll and told him I would be back to pay him the last penny. He stood there with mouth open and his tongue hanging out. I learned a lot that day. Assert yourself!

A week later, a very good friend of mine from high school called and told me that he was getting divorced. He and his wife were one of the two married couples who were in our group when we were in Los Angeles for the first two years. While I was in the Army, one couple had moved to Boston and Louis and Joan moved to New Hampshire. Now unfortunately, Louis was returning to Los Angeles and asked if I was going home for Christmas. I told him I couldn't leave because I was doing a show until New Year's Eve, which thankfully was true. "We could go together," he said. He changed his plans and we left January 4th through the heavy snowstorms in upstate New York. We got to Vegas and had planned to sleep in the desert so that we could save our money and go to see Peggy Lee's ten o'clock show and then go to Sinatra's midnight show. It was about five in the afternoon and we drove out a couple of miles from Vegas and tried to sleep in the car. It was so hot we lasted about a half hour. We went to one of the hotels to get cooled off but now we were hungry. We tried to figure out how to get one burger for the two of us. We planned the drinks (two-drink minimum). I don't remember a cover charge. If there was a cover charge, we planned it into the budget. Bottom line: after Sinatra we could only afford to buy gas. That way we could drive straight to Los Angeles and eat at my house. We hung around until about eight o'clock at which time we were sleeping in the car out in the desert, only this time we were freezing. So, forget Peggy Lee and forget Sinatra. We drove out of town where the prices were cheaper and we ate like pigs. Then we drove to Los Angeles and even stopped for a cup of coffee.

Chapter 25

I went to my parents' house and in time we solved the problem they had spoken about. I decided to stay in L.A. for a while to see what was happening. It was funny. I was making plans but other things were coming. One of the girls in my acting class was dating a film producer and he was making a film and asked if I would I like to be in it and get my Screen Actors Guild card. Yes to all of the above. Now I believed Hemingway's line to "let life happen to you." I got my SAG card and continued doing small parts in mostly small movies. But, I was learning a lot. In the first film I did, I was on a forty-foot tower and I was getting shot with an arrow. We rehearsed it and then we were ready to shoot. Before I got shot, someone had a line, "Here comes a wagon." The guy saying it said, "Here come the wagons." The director yelled cut and said, "No. No. Here comes *A* wagon. There's only one wagon coming. Okay?" The guy said, "Okay!" So we got going again and everyone was in a hurry because we had almost lost the sun, which was necessary to match. The director called, "Action," and we hear the line, "Here comes *A* wagon," emphasizing, of course, the *A* since it was only one wagon.

Finally, we got it done and then the camera turns on me as I start to speak, and before I can speak I get an arrow in the back. There was no arrow as we were doing the long shot now and the close-up the next day with a flaming arrow. Acting as if I got shot from behind, I leaned over the tower railing and proceeded to die. But, I realized that my hat was falling off. So, being a good soldier, I tried to catch it before it hit the ground. I caught it and put it on my head and then continued to die. I hate to tell you what happened then. We had to shoot both of my scenes the next day. That didn't sit too well with anybody, except the actors who would get paid for an extra day.

The flaming arrow shot. I had a square piece of balsa wood tied to my back by means of four leather straps. One strap on every corner. There was horsehair filament attached to the center of the balsa wood. This filament passed through my shirt and ended up, off camera, with the man who would light the arrow and then release the spring that would send the arrow into the balsa wood. The arrow was shot and it was done in one take. The director came over to me. He had told me previously not to stand up or my hair would burn. When he came over to me, I was in my "burning" dead position. He patted my head and said, "You more than made up for yesterday, kid. You did a great job and in one take." I thought, "One take. Man, I'm Brando." Meanwhile, I am waiting for them to come and put out the fire. I'm waiting, and waiting, and waiting. Now it's getting hotter and hotter. Did they say to wait? Maybe I made a mistake. But I feel very hot. But it's July and it's hot. And this is my first movie and they told me today how good I was. I am thrilled until I hear someone say, "Hey, the kid's on fire." That's why I was hot. Then I felt the bucket of water which was thrown at me. I figured maybe I should go into comedy. My back was burned like I had a bad sunburn. But I was okay.

When members of the press visited the set, I was introduced as "one of the fastest rising young stars in Hollywood." Maybe that's why I tried to keep my hat on. I wanted to look good for the close-ups. I began to think that maybe I was hot. But I wasn't getting any work, so that thought disappeared quickly. For that first movie, I got very good money. When I showed my check to my father he asked what that was for and I told him for a week's work on a movie. He said, "Just for acting?" "Yes Pa," I said, "They pay good money but only the big stars work a lot and get more money." (What am I, a prophet?) He didn't trust it and told me to wait and see what happens. Cut to about six months later. A movie is planned, I go to a location in another state near California, our first check bounces, and we never get a second check. I called home and said, "Pa, send me $20 to come home." He sent it and when I got home, I told him what had happened. He said, "I told you that movies are no good. First they pay you and then you pay them."

I explained but he wouldn't hear of it. He told me that I should go get a real job.

When I had first gone to New York I wrote a letter to Elia Kazan and told him the following: "I am Greek and you are Greek and I think you should help me get started. Sincerely, Gene Chronopoulos" He sent me to a producer's office and casting director, but they said I was too young for anything going on at that time. The casting director said he would call and he did call a couple of months later and again I was too young because the part called for the actor to understudy two other small parts but older characters. By this time, I was supposed to do a TV show in three weeks. One week before that, the show went off the air. I auditioned prior to that for a showcase and sang *Body and Soul* and *Mountain Greenery*. They liked me and I sang another song. When they called me back, they called to say the club I was supposed to sing at had closed. I checked and it was true. Now, before I left for L.A. with Louis, I went to see Elia Kazan. He said, "Why are you going to Hollywood?" I told him there were some family things and they need me there. He said, "They won't know what to do with you. You have intelligent eyes and a baby face." He was nice enough to give me a letter to Jeff Corey. Jeff Corey was a blacklisted actor to whom many studios sent their "pretty" people to learn how to act, like someone who had just gotten the lead in a major movie but who had no acting experience whatsoever. Jeff had a great reputation with all the major studios. When I returned to Los Angeles, the first thing I did was to go see Jeff Corey. (This was before the movie, which I was not aware of at the time.) I remember our conversation. After a few minutes of talking about the theater, acting, and the importance of the arts on social, philosophical and political views, he asked me:

> Jeff: Do you think you are a good actor?
> Gene: Yes.
> Jeff: Then why do you want to come to my class?
> Gene: Because I want to become a better actor.
> Jeff: Why?
> Gene: I want to make people think just as the ancient Greek tragedies did.
> Jeff: Our new classes start in six weeks.

> Gene: When do I audition?
> Jeff: No audition. You're in.

I was of course in heaven. To study with Jeff Corey was a dream come true. We had all heard about him. We talked a bit more about my last statement. I told him that I had learned about the Greek theater from my father and that he said it demanded a desire to make the world a better place, to teach people to have empathy, to help them get through their problems more easily. He called the theater "the mirror of society." Thankfully, Jeff Corey was the best coach ever!

Chapter 26

Through a friend of mine, I got a job at RCA pressing records. It was a night shift. From midnight to 7 A.M. I think we also got a half-hour break but I really don't remember. The job was boring but most of the people working there were actors so conversations were great and we learned about who was casting what. You would face a machine, which had two arms. With both hands you would push the two arms forward until they stopped. A stream of tar-like vinyl would come down onto the platen. While the vinyl was coming out, you would take a label with each hand and place one up and one down on the turntable. Then you would put the vinyl in the middle of the bottom turntable and press the two arms of this machine. You would do the same on the other side and then you would turn to the first turntable. By now the first record was pressed. You would then place the pressed record on a higher-level turntable and while it trimmed the records, you would be back starting a new record. Boring? Then, continue again. Isn't that nice? I thought you'd like to know how it's done.

The money was good, which paid for classes although sleep was lacking. The crowning glory of this job was that they pressed records for some jazz record companies. Primarily, Contemporary Records, which had Shelly Manne and Chico Hamilton on drums, Buddy Collett on flute and reeds, Hampton Hawes on piano, Art Pepper on alto sax, LeRoy Vinnegar on bass, Sonny Rollins on tenor sax, Ray Brown on bass, Barney Kessel on guitar, Cecil Taylor on piano, and even Ornette Coleman on various instruments. Many years later, when I bartended at private parties, I ran into Buddy Collette on numerous occasions and we talked about all the good times we had.

There were always extra records made to cover shortages, errors on the label, or various other mistakes. When the records were all pressed and checked and the numbers were correct, they would give some away to the workers. The jazz records pressed were few. Mostly, the records were RCA. I remember they gave me Belafonte and Lena Horne and not much else. All RCA wanted was the pop LPs of the day. There were some Verve pressed there, although I don't remember anyone getting any of the Verve or Clef; these were all Norman Granz companies. We did press the Fred Astaire set with Astaire tap dancing with the backing of the JATP All-Stars and Annie Ross' *Gypsy* on World Pacific. I never got those so I bought Annie Ross and years later got the Fred Astaire as a gift. The LP that they did give me was Annie Ross with Gerry Mulligan, which was awesome. I will always love Annie in addition to her marvelous singing because she was one of the few who supported Billie and visited her when she was in her last days. And when they finally put a star on Hollywood Boulevard for Billie, it was Annie who said, "Every girl singer should get down on her knees and thank God that there was a Billie Holiday." That also goes for the long list of male singers and musicians who fell under the magic and genius of Lady Day.

When Billie Holiday starred in a jazz concert at the Hollywood Bowl, I bought a ticket and went. That's right. One ticket and even that was hard to obtain. After a couple of performers had appeared, I saw what I had been eyeballing since I got there. And that was the box seats, which were way down front. I really can't remember when I decided to move into those seats because I saw that one of the boxes had six seats and only two were taken. After the first two acts, I walked down to the box seats during some heavy applause. I held my ticket in my hand, looking at it, and mumbled about being sorry I was late and took a seat. I thought that the chance of these seats being taken was rare since they were empty from the start of the concert. I looked around and I was surprised to see so many celebrities. I was not impressed because I was waiting to hear Lady Day sing. It was only later that I realized that I was sitting next to two people whom I have always loved and admired, Humphrey Bogart and Lauren Bacall, who were sitting in the box on my right. I spoke with Bogart during the intermission about the performances and Billie, in particular. It wasn't really a conversation, just some talk between jazz fans. And I never told him I was a Scotch drinker because of him. I was cool. But I did tell him that he was my favorite actor.

According to the notes on the new Billie Holiday LP, it was recorded on the Monday following this Saturday night concert. It was called *Music For Torching* and named Record of the Year by METRONOME Magazine. DOWNBEAT gave it five stars and said, "No one is able to touch Billie as the most emotionally striking singer in jazz, twenty years ago or today. Totally recommended." George Wein, the owner of Storyville in Boston, wrote an article about being asked who his favorites were. In the Boston Globe entitled: "BILLIE HOLIDAY IS BEST OF PAST, PRESENT SINGERS" he wrote in part: "When I am home by myself, or with close friends, and not concerned with listening to records as a reviewer, or for academic purposes, but only want to hear music that makes me feel good, I play Billie Holiday. She is my favorite."

Ella Fitzgerald explained this influence in an interview in 1990. "I idolized Billie and her songs. But Billie wasn't like what people say. She was like that because of her songs, not the other way around. She was the first really modern singer to my way of thinking. We all wanted to be like her."

Two more albums were released on the Verve label called *Velvet Mood* and *Lady Sings The Blues* and both received ratings of five stars. I had just purchased them and was slated to leave for New York for an audition. So I got to hear these two LPs only once or twice but I can still remember the impact of *I Don't Want to Cry Anymore*, *What's New* and *I Thought About You*. The latter had only Bobby Tucker backing Billie on piano. The lyrics:

"I peeked through the crack
And I looked at the track
The one going back to you
And what did I do?
I thought about you."

You can visualize every action she sings in this part of the song. Just after that, an album entitled *Body and Soul* got a three and one half star from Don Gold in DOWNBEAT. I was ready to burst. I was used to seeing her five stars in practically everything she did for Verve; the reissues from Decca, Columbia, and Commodore drew raves; and now a three and a half star? I wrote a letter to DOWNBEAT, which they printed. Of course it was not good. I was only a kid.

Here is my letter in its entirety:

A Sad Day?...

New York City
To The Editor:

Don Gold's review of Billie Holiday's new LP is the worst I've ever read! He always seemed to be a critic of the "knock-em-down-pick-them-up a-little" school, but proved it with this review. He's the type of critic who feels so important, he can say anything. Cutting down Lady is like cutting down Duke, Satch, Bird, Pres, etc. What these people are to their respective instruments and Duke to his band and his composing, Lady is to jazz singing. Although she is not the same singer she was 20 years ago, she's not worse!

For your information, Mr. Gold, Lady can out-project any pop or jazz singer in the field! As for Lady being coarse, never! And as for her voice "technically", a true critic would never take this into consideration of a jazz performance. After all, Satch and Lee Wiley, among other jazz singers leave much to be desired technically – but not emotionally! And no singer today has the true emotion, beat, extraordinary phrasing, that Lady has! And don't mention these other so-called jazz singers to me! The jazz singers of today can be counted on the fingers of one hand. Many sing with a jazz feeling but to be a true jazz singer you need all that Lady has.

As one critic said, "If you want to know what jazz is all about – listen to Billie Holiday. And so many other true critics, musicians, and fans have said so much about Lady it would be useless to reiterate. Suffice it to say, you should take lessons, Mr. Gold, from Hentoff, Feather, Ulanov, and Coss. Also, read some foreign jazz critics' remarks on Lady! I thought just the fans here were useless as far as jazz singing goes, but I see some so-called critics are the same! But then I'd put you in the class of fans who think jazz started in 1950. I'm only 22 but I've gone back and listened to all eras of jazz. Maybe you should do the same!

The World's Greatest
Billie Holiday Fan,
Evgenios Chronopoulos

Chapter 27

One night, I was walking home in New York City and I ran into Lady and Louis McKay on 42nd Street near 8th Avenue. It seems whenever I wrote something about her, I saw her. This was the time that I told her about the letter I wrote and she said, "Honey, I'm singing better than ever now. I don't know why they're sayin' that. They're always sayin' I'm coming back. I honestly don't know where in the hell I've been." She sometimes said, "I've been nowhere but across town." She wrote that same thing in an article once and I laughed about it. While we were talking, Louis McKay went to get her the hot dog she had asked for earlier. Just talking to Billie was a thrill. She was honest and intelligent and she was never anything but kind and warm to a kid who loved her and her music.

We talked about the letter, which I had written to DOWNBEAT about the *Body and Soul* LP. I signed it "Evgenios Chronopoulos, the World's Greatest Billie Holiday Fan." I did that because I had written to so many different magazines and didn't want them to see the same name over and over. So I thought I'd use my Greek name, so as to seem to be a different person than the one whose letters were published. They printed the letter and I got calls from everyone in town saying they dug it. Someone answered the letter and I answered him but they did not print my response.

Lady sang at the concert in Central Park called "Jazz Under the Stars." She sang so beautifully that night and I wondered how she could make everything sound so personal. It was understandable in smaller clubs, but the huge space of Central Park condensed itself into a Billie

Holiday arena. After the show at Central Park, I tried to go backstage to see her but the crowds were so huge that I had to do an end run around the crowd. I ended up on the path leading to Central Park West and coming from my left, down another little path, was Lady Day. My first thought was, "Here is the world's greatest jazz singer walking through Central Park, alone." I shouted, "Lady." She turned as I ran toward her and hugged her. As I did, I thought, "This is really the first time I've touched her." We said our hello's, etc., discussed her performance and then we talked about the movie of her life that she was doing and for which she was going to sing the soundtrack. She really wanted to do it, she told me. I asked who was going to play her.

She said she wanted Ava Gardner but that Ava wouldn't be available due to previous commitments, so they were looking for someone else. I mentioned one name. "No, honey, she can't play me. She's a cold bitch. I don't care if she's black or not, but she has to be warm. Ava is warm."

I mentioned a couple of others and they were both wrong in her mind. I have read from various sources that she didn't want Ava Gardner but only Ken Vail prints the story in his "Lady Day's Diary" closest to the way that Billie told it to me. She never mentioned Lana Turner either, which in itself was ludicrous, but still it was printed in various places. We walked and talked until we got to Central Park West. She hailed a cab and said, "I'll be back, honey." As the song goes, "Every time we say goodbye, I die a little." This may sound dramatic, but it is nonetheless true. I never knew when I would see her again.

Back to Los Angeles and walking through Beverly Hills, I saw Gerry Mulligan with Judy Holiday, who he was dating at the time. They made an album together which was really quite good. We talked about the days at The Haig being one of those golden moments in one's life. Not because of the success, which of course was richly deserved and welcomed, but because of the feeling of appreciation of the music and also of the artist who created those great moments. How truly human he was and how good it was to see him again. The last time I saw him was at a gig at UCLA, and each time it was like seeing an old friend – not a major jazz musician and celebrity.

I owed him so much. One day when I was out of cigarettes, I went down to his apartment and asked him for a cigarette. As I was looking at him going to get the cigarette, I spotted some pot on the table right in front of me. I asked if I could have "one of these." Emphatically and with a little anger, he said: "No! And if you ever start that stuff, I'll never talk to you again." He knew that I would listen to him. That was it for me. Many years later, Lady told me something like that which was much more personal. With all the drugs floating around in those years, it is a wonder that I never used anything. I was getting high on the music, something that a lot of the people around me could not understand. But I had seen so much of what drugs could do to someone that it scared me and I was old enough to know that I should be scared.

Two new jazz clubs opened in Hollywood diagonally across from each other. They were called Jazz City and Peacock Alley. I would go into these clubs and sit at the bar. This way I would only have to buy one drink. I became the kind of guy I hated when I was bartending. But my funds were low. (But I always left a good tip.)

Shelly Manne also opened a club in the middle of Hollywood. That's where I got to see the groups of Bill Evans on piano, Charlie Byrd on guitar, Terry Gibbs on vibes, Gene Harris on piano, and his Three Sounds, Stan Gets on tenor sax, and singer Astrud Gilberto at the height of the bossa nova craze. It was a happening place and in the middle of Hollywood. It was called Shelly's Manhole. It lasted long enough to become a strong and delicious memory of an almost perfect jazz club.

Chapter 28

The ads were all over town that the great Lady Day was coming to Jazz City for two weeks. What an opening. All I could get was a seat at the bar. I didn't see her after the show because her dressing room was packed with people including many celebrities. But every night after that until she closed, I was there. For the next two weeks, I saw both of her sets every night, and spent time in her dressing room between sets with her primarily, but also with her husband, Louis McKay, who was there almost every night.

About three or four nights later when I stayed, I asked Louis if I could stay with Billie in the dressing room. He said that would be great because he could leave the club every so often as he had many things to do. I gave her a small wallet-sized picture of the one we took at the Hi-Hat in Boston.

The first night that I was there, I asked Billie if I could bring in my copy of her biography so that she could sign it. She said, "Sure, honey."

"Can I bring in my camera so we can take some pictures?" I asked.

She said, "Bring it in and we'll spend some time together."

What I remember most about those nights, is the varied conversations about many things happening in music, in the world, in her life and in her career. I think the strong link was the picture that we had taken together at the Hi-Hat in Boston. That's when she had her dog Chiquita. At this time, she had a new Chihuahua called Pepito. At one point, she had both of them there until Chiquita passed away.

It was a few years after Chet Baker had his hit with *My Funny Valentine*. I asked her why she didn't record it.

"Do you think I can sing it, honey?"

I said, surprised, "You can sing anything, Billie!!"

On another night a songwriter came around and wanted her to see a song he had written. He had knocked on the door and when I opened it he handed me a piece of sheet music. I gave it to Billie and when she had looked at it, she said, "What the hell is this? *Loneliness is a Well.*"

As she handed back the sheet music, she asked me what I thought of it. "I don't read music," I said.

She said, "Forget the music. Look at those words." That told me so much! She could handle the melody, she could fix that if it wasn't to her liking, but the lyrics, she couldn't change those very much. She couldn't feel them. The songwriter, of course, was waiting outside the door. I told her I was no expert so I didn't know if it was good or bad. She asked me if the songwriter was still outside. I told her that he was still waiting. I went outside and told him that Billie would get back to him. I gave him the sheet music and he gave me his business card which I gave to Lady. Years later, on an Anita O'Day album called *Live at Mr. Kelly's,* I heard the song and had to agree with Billie; it was not for her.

She said, "Do you know that they once brought me *How Much is That Doggie in the Window*? Look at Patti Page. She took it and made a million dollars. I should have done it. She sings like me, anyway!"

Another day, I got to the club earlier than usual so that we could take pictures. We didn't have a chance prior to that. So this particular night, we took pictures in her dressing room and then during her second set, I was able to take two pictures of her while she was singing. Thankfully, no one's head got in the way. She was full of passion in every song that night.

Gardenias were delivered every night. Rosemary Clooney and Jose Ferrer had sent them on opening night when they went to see Billie. They continued sending them throughout her two-week engagement. She was as happy as a child when she was telling me the story. I was so happy for Lady because her moments of happiness were so few. I heard many of those sad stories or read about them. Thankfully, for these two weeks, Lady was very happy. As a result, she was in great shape every night. The crowds were there cheering and it added to her joy. During the first week of her stay, she had appeared on the television show *Stars of Jazz* and the club started getting busier and busier because of that appearance.

In all the times I had seen Billie perform, I had never heard her sing *Strange Fruit*. We had discussed it earlier in the week. I told her I'd like to hear her sing it in person. She said she couldn't do that song easily. It hurt her too much. But I was still happy with whatever she sang.

As I had promised her, I brought my mother to meet her. We had talked about mothers and she wanted to meet mine. I told Billie that my mother spoke very little English but she said she didn't care. I told Billie that whenever I played her records at home, my mother would say, "That's Billie." She got a big kick out of that.

On one of my trips to Greece, I picked up a book on jazz written in Greek that explained many things, including the genius of Lady Day. I gave it to my mother who read it and said, "Now I know who Billie is and why she sings the way she does." And so, Lady and my mother and her limited English finally met. They got along very well with very little help from me. They talked about music and about cooking. My mother was a great cook and tried to tell Billie about Greek food. She and Billie exchanged thoughts of the kind of food they liked to cook and it was really a scene to behold. The time came to leave and we said goodbye. My mother said, "Billie, you sing beautiful," and holding her heart she said, "Apo Tho" (Greek for "from here.")

Billie said, "Take care of your mama. You only have one. I lost mine and now I'm all alone." It was very moving. I didn't want to leave just then, and I think that Billie understood. She was really very intelligent about human behavior and said, "You coming tomorrow, honey?" I said, "Billie, you didn't have to ask. I told you I'd be here every night." The look on her face was spine tingling.

We smiled at each other and I took my mother home. The next night I was there, of course, right on time and the deliveryman handed me the gardenias, having seen me so many times in the dressing room. I took them in to Billie and she smiled so sweetly, again like a little child.

A few nights later, after another great set, she sang *Strange Fruit*, and when she finished she left the stage crying. We went into her dressing room. She continued to cry deeply. I put my arms around her and hugged her. I tried to say soothing words, but I can't remember what I said. I was crying, too. But as I drew back I saw the teardrops, which had fallen onto her gown. It was a velvet burgundy colored gown with a square neck, and the teardrops looked like drops of blood on the dress. I have collected many pictures of Lady over the years, and I have never seen that gown in any of those pictures. I don't know why, but I just find it strange. I feel it was a special occasion just for me. Corny? Maybe. But very memorable. That scene was so vivid; it's imprinted on my brain, never to be forgotten. For those who say she didn't know what she was singing about when she sang the song, or as others have said that she didn't care about the song, I never believed it when I first read it, and now I know it's not so. When Billie sang *Strange Fruit*, it was tantamount to a protest against racism. I know that Billie was a very strong woman. How else can one explain how she survived all 44 years of her life with all the injustices she had to endure. I have also found out that the strongest women are also the most vulnerable.

Two more nights and the engagement was over. Two great sets including *Porgy* in both sets on that last night. Then the time came to say goodbye to Lady and Louis McKay. I was sad to see her leave. But I also was happy that I was blessed to have been able to spend all that time with her. I got my fill but only for a short time. Very soon I missed seeing her, even though I listened to her records every day to remind me of her genius and her beautiful soul.

Chapter 29

There were many good jazz artists in the late fifties, and if they came to Los Angeles, I saw them. I loved that jazz corner on Hollywood Boulevard and Western Avenue. I always saw great musicians there. One night, I went to see the Modern Jazz Quartet at Jazz City, and when they were on a break, I ran across the street to see Dizzy Gillespie's band and Carmen McRae. Dizzy's band played *Manteca* and *Salt Peanuts,* which I knew, along with others that were new to me. *Manteca* ran about ten minutes and the joint was jumping.

When I was growing up in New Hampshire, Dizzy Gillespie joined with musicians from Cuba and helped create Afro-Cuban jazz. I guess every era has its Luciano, but in my youth it was Luciano Pozo y Gonzalos who played amazing conga drums as well as other percussion instruments. He was called Chano Pozo and his playing on conga drums was a sensation in addition to composing songs including *Manteca*, which he composed with Dizzie Gillespie and Gil Fuller. Manteca is still being played today but the original version with Chano Pozo is the one that I dig the most. In our teens as we were growing up, Afro-Cuban music, as well as the dancers, was very thrilling and exciting to us.

I used to want to scat so I scatted with all those great Bop records. But I could never do *The Champ*. At the club that night, I asked Diz how to do *The Champ*, which was his tune. I told him I could do *Move* by Miles, and I did it for him. We were at the end of the bar and he slammed his hand on the bar, which scared me, and he went "da ra da ra da ra da – da ra dara." So for years, that was the only way I could do *The Champ*, by slapping my hand on a hard surface. But at first, as

I said, he scared me. I thought he was angry, but when he started to scat, I knew it was OK. I went in again a few days later, and again sat at the bar. Suddenly, someone's hand came in front of me and slammed the bar. It was Diz. He pointed at me as if to say, "Take it!" and I went into *The Champ*. I have never forgotten it. I will also never forget the great Dizzy Gillespie not only for his music but also for his kindness, humor and humanity. He had a heart as big as Jupiter and he was very, very funny.

Carmen came on and did a beautiful set. I kept calling out for *If I'm Lucky* from her *Easy to Love* album. She did her set and two encores. She started to leave the stage; when she got closer to me, I said with a sad face, "*If I'm Lucky*"! She stopped and went back and sang it. How do you forget people like that? Always giving and mostly getting very little in return…

Billie was never far from my mind. The arguments and misinformation continued, but then something happened that made people lay flowers at her feet. It was Sunday, and a friend of mine who lived in the Bronx invited me to dinner. I had met her through the man who hired me to translate for the Greek Seaman's Union in New York. That was another way I was supporting myself. I didn't own a TV set, so I really didn't hear the promos for upcoming programs. When I got to the Bronx where my friend Helen lived, I went upstairs, rang the bell, and when she answered the door, she was holding a scotch on the rocks for me. I went in and sat down to watch the news, while she prepared dinner. It was about 2:30 in the afternoon. There was a break in the news, and they announced that the *Seven Lively Arts* special for this Sunday was *The Sound of Jazz*. Great! Then he announced the musicians who would appear. I went crazy when I heard Billie Holiday's name and I yelled. Helen ran out of the kitchen to see what had happened. I explained very little because I had something like three hours to announce it to the whole country. I called a friend in New York and told him to call everybody he knew. I did the same to my cousin in New Jersey and an Army buddy in Jersey (the famous Rick from Germany), and then realized that I was calling long distance. I placed a call to my sister, collect, and told her about the show and tried to get the calls that I had made put onto my phone in Los Angeles. It was denied, but I made it up to Helen later. She said, "Forget it." But when you are so broke that you miss meals, and someone invites you to dinner, then it really is appreciated. You can never do enough for people like that.

As stated earlier, Billie could not sing in any New York club that served liquor, so the only place to hear her was on radio or in a concert hall, which was too expensive for me. I sat and relished the hour and also saw my friend Gerry Mulligan, my favorite baritone sax man, Lester Young, my favorite soloist, and all the other greats. Most agreed that this was the finest hour of jazz ever presented on national television. Billie had the ideal setting: jazz musicians who loved her and most of whom she had worked with before. She was magnificent, as anyone who saw the show, I'm sure, will agree. She sang *Fine and Mellow* in great voice, and with all the other attributes of which she possessed more than any other vocalist.

When the LP of the show came out, it was not entirely as exciting as it was on television. I thought it was because we saw the musicians on TV but not on the record. I found out years later that I was wrong. The LP is from the rehearsal four days earlier. That's why Gerry Mulligan's name is not listed on the LP credits. I thought it was because he had a recording contract with another company. Sometime later, with the arrival of video, the show became available for everyone to see a living document of life being lived by a great artist.

Billie sang with her whole body the way she was when one saw her in clubs. And you will hear Lester Young in what one critic called the most pure blues he ever heard: Roy Eldridge and Doc Cheatham on trumpet, Vic Dickinson on trombone, Lester Young, Coleman Hawkins, and Ben Webster on tenor sax, Gerry Mulligan on baritone sax, Mal Waldron on piano, Danny Barker on guitar, Milt Hinton on bass, and Jo Jones on drums. Here's a chance to start discovering these great artists on albums of their own, and I promise you, they'll lead you to some magnificent and thrilling sounds. Billie's singing and Lester Young's blues solo on this TV show is monumental music.

I stayed in New York for a year or so working and studying. I had met a couple who were writers and we started hanging out together, mostly on weekends. Together with my two friends from Los Angeles, we were all invited to their home for dinner on a Saturday night. We had never talked jazz with Danny and Inez, but prominently situated in their home was a picture of Billie Holiday looking very beautiful.

Upon further examination I discovered that it was an LP called *Lady in Satin*. They told me that they didn't know her but that someone had touted them onto this LP. Being in the financial position I was in, I hadn't even heard of this recording.

These were the moments when not having any money and struggling to get ahead in the theater upset me. I had no money for magazines and reviews. I was busy trying merely to pay the rent and eat so I missed buying this album, just as I had missed out on the concert at Town Hall. If I had been in Los Angeles, it wouldn't have bothered me, but being in New York and not being able to see Billie really was a drag. I couldn't afford to buy this LP, although I knew that in time I would have to get it. About that there was no question. We listened to the record and the feeling was so intense it made me shiver. It was so completely moving my first thought was that the detractors would now say that the voice was gone. The voice indeed had lost much of its power, but now her phrasing and articulation and her love of lyrics were more evident. She created a whole new dimension of Billie Holiday. When the album was reviewed, Bill Coss in METRONOME wrote: "…such jazz soloists as trombonists Urbie Green and J.J. Johnson, trumpeter Mel Davis, by arranger Ray Ellis, who Billie especially wanted for this album. Listeners who are frightened with the prospect of Billie and Strings may be calmed by the thought of her recordings on Decca with Bob Haggart's arrangements. Here, as there, the conventional instrumentation heightens the peculiar Holiday sound the way that marmalade and mustard in the right combination can produce the wildest barbecue sauce for ribs, and this particular product of Adam's last rib is set off in just such a way, and for me, as for Nat Hentoff, Billie can hardly do wrong, and I have a tendency to write off my own enthusiasm for her singing as overpowering bias, but I feel that most listeners will agree with me here that if Billie's powers are in any kind of eclipse, they are considerably charmed into shape by everything surrounding them, and although I know there is a better Billie available, I continue to insist that this is a Holiday-fare of fine quality." Bill Coss, who reviewed the album, being one of our best jazz critics, I think was the proper person to quote because *Lady in Satin* started the old clichés about her "decline" again.

It is surprising to my friends in film and theater that some of the clippings that I have in my scrapbook on Billie Holiday come from some pretty far out sources. Now, who would think to find a record review of a jazz artist in PHOTOPLAY Magazine? One friend asked me how I can always demand that the work comes first and the celebrity can come later, and to not think about it, even if it does come. He asked, "You go and buy a PHOTOPLAY Magazine?" I explained that when I am at newsstands, I somehow gravitate to magazines for no reason at all, and then I find a review like this: "*Lady in Satin,* Billie Holiday with Ray Ellis and his orchestra. Billie Holiday is back on records and we're glad. Her voice seems to have mellowed with the years and the lush string backgrounds with voices and jazz solos here and there are definitely a new setting for this great jazz singer. We remember her in the early days of her career with the Basie band…. How about following up *Lady in Satin* with *Lady with Basie?*" Where did he think she was for about 20 years? With the comment, "Billie is back on records," the reviewer begs that question. For whatever reason, many people simply did not know that she was still singing in clubs around the country with occasional concert hall performances in New York City.

♪

Chapter 30

I loved reading the reviews from around the country. From San Francisco, "Billie Holiday's three day stand at the Black Hawk was the biggest draw the club has ever had. Capacity and turn-away crowds for all shows." From Washington, DC, "Billie Holiday did triple encores during her appearance at the Patio Lounge…the applause shook the rafters." I think one would have to have been around in the middle to late fifties in order to know what was happening in the jazz singer's world. The new singers were all to some degree or another copying Billie. The established stars were on the fence between jazz and pop, and Billie remained the uncompromising jazz singer. This is not to put anyone down. Jazz was never the popular music of America, so to make a living, many singers went to Japan and Europe where they were treated as artists. It's what Billie had said upon her return to the States after her tour of Europe. Many articles were being written about who was and who wasn't a jazz singer. So, for me, it was a time when there were more articles about Billie, which pleased me no end.

A new Verve LP named *Songs for Distingue Lovers* was released and Jack Tracy said in DOWNBEAT: "Miss Holiday remains the unique stylist, still incomparable. But the vocal power and vitality is not what it used to be. Had this set been recorded…ten years ago, the album could have been a jazz milestone." We all change and evolve, but we hear this album today and it still is very close to a jazz milestone. Also, it is selling to a whole new generation of listeners.

While it is true that Billie Holiday's voice was not the same in the fifties as it was in the thirties and forties, it is also true that the genius (a very over-used word) and the soul (another over-used word) and the originality that no one could ever duplicate was simply the evolution of a jazz singer and a human being. She always sang as she felt. Tempos would change, but the impact of her feeling never did. Some musicians think that the sides made in her last decade are better than the earlier ones. I think we should just enjoy them as we hear all the eras and changes in the life of a magnificent artist. Someone said that she sang that way because of the bad breaks in her life. I disagree. Many people have suffered, but they could not convey that suffering to others. That takes an artist, a singer, and a great actress. As writer and critic Martin Williams has said, "She was an actress but she never had an act." Instead, she had a voice that could convey all of the feelings found in humanity. The French actress, Jeanne Moreau said that Billie put more emotion into a three-minute song than most actresses do in a three-act play.

Decca started to release Lady's records on LP albums. The people who had not seen her perform for many years in New York wrote her off as a has-been. And the people who read that she was not performing well got a surprise if they read the reviews, or better still, listened to the records which few did. Some would even dismiss the reviews as "nostalgia." They dismissed these sides as inferior, but Glenn Coulter, in the JAZZ REVIEW wrote: "It seems wasteful to attempt description of these performances: anybody of a certain age must have taken cognizance of them when they were first issued…what was not so apparent when they were released two by two was their expressive variety: the cold dismissal of *No More*, the contorted pathos of *You Better Go Now*, the perhaps excessive virtuosity of *Ain't Nobody's Business. I'll Look Around* is a lesson for all who would be jazz singers, the line sustained from first to last, the approach to it just suspenseful enough to make it live, the words forced to generate real meaning. But there is no pat explanation of how Billie can make a quite common interval, say a major third, seem an unusual and difficult leap, nor of how she can isolate and break down for analysis the counter words in her lyrics."

Of the reissued Commodore sides, he wrote, "…Even God tires of too much alleluia, and it would be fruitless to invent fresh ways of commending performances which Commodore rightly calls 'classic.'"

In the JAZZ REVIEW, when asked whether he agreed with most of the writers on jazz that the Billie of 20 years ago was the "best Billie, and that she is now in a decline," Miles Davis said, "I'd rather hear her now. She's become much more mature. Sometimes you can sing words every night for five years, and all of a sudden it dawns on you what the song means. I played *My Funny Valentine* for a long time and didn't like it, and all of a sudden it meant something. So with Billie, you know she's not thinking now what she was in 1937, and she probably learned more about different things. And, she still has control, probably more control now than then. No, I don't think she's in a decline. What I like about Billie is that she sings it just the way she hears it and that's usually the way best suited for her. She has more feeling than Ella and more experience in living a certain way than Ella. Billie's pretty wild, you know. She sings way behind the beat and then she brings it up—hitting right on the beat. You can play behind the beat, but every once in a while you have to cut into the rhythm section on the beat and that keeps everybody together. Sinatra does it by accenting a word. A lot of singers try to sing like Billie, but just the act of playing behind the beat doesn't make it sound soulful. I don't think that guys like Buck Clayton are the best possible accompanists for her. I'd rather hear her with Bobby Tucker, the pianist she used to have. She doesn't need any horns, she sounds like one, anyway."

September 1958 was the evening of a concert at Town Hall in New York where Billie sang. John S. Wilson in the NEW YORK TIMES wrote, "…she eased into a swinging version of *When Your Lover Has Gone*, and some of the old Holiday magic began to peep through. This magic has been hard to come by for Miss Holiday in recent years. But it grew and grew…by the time she wound up with *Billie's Blues*, she was singing with more assurance, skill and spirit than this listener has heard from her in years" (and he lived in New York). Also, in September when she sang at the "Jazz at the Plaza" party for Columbia Records, she sang *When Your Lover has Gone* and then went into *Don't Explain*. I think it is the best version of that song. The reaction of the crowd is enough to tell you how good she was. The bridge is one of the best examples of her vocal power at this time. She ends it as never before and it is startling in its beauty.

Again in September, at the Seven Ages of Jazz Festival in Wallingford, Connecticut, she was superb. One critic wrote that the festival was only marred by the Billie Holiday vocals but others felt differently. "Critics lately have praised her for showing 'flashes of the old brilliance' so frequently that one might well mistake hers for the eternal fire of the Arc de Triomphe," wrote Glen Coulter in the JAZZ REVIEW. After commenting on one of her albums which was not to his liking, he states, "Billie's superiority (I am sure it remains), and will remain after this record has been deleted, has always rested in transcending her materials, hacking off melodic excess, and attacking the words with, alternately, deeper conviction and greater contempt."

Jazz singing is a very special art, and the singer must deal with all that a musician deals with but must also have to deal with the lyrics. You have to convey a story and do it while you are improvising to enhance the lyric not merely to change it. Billie's greatness and genius lay in the fact that when she improvised she enhanced the lyric while many lesser singers improvised the music while losing the story line. In ESQUIRE Magazine in January 1959, Harold Hayes wrote an article entitled:

"Billie Holiday She remains, in 1959 as in 1939, superbly immediate"

"…what she (Billie) has more than any other…is style…in such abundance and used so skillfully that the listener is conscious only of the emotions she wishes to convey: infinite tenderness, utter futility, desperate gaiety and nasty resentment. The blues are hers, and when she sings them, there can be no doubt in the heart of the listener that it is bound to rain for some time." He continues with, "It would be a discredit to Miss Holiday and Pecksniffian criticism to suggest one record of hers over another. Therefore, her latest fourteen albums." He lists all fourteen and closes with, "Gold never came so cheap."

On the cover of METRONOME Magazine, February 1959—Billie Holiday. Survey of Jazz Singers. Opening to the first page is a beautiful picture of Billie with the caption, "Billie Holiday, the one singer who always sings jazz."

"FACTS & FALLACIES" – by George O. Von Frank

Mr. Von Frank listed seven criteria as prerequisites to being a jazz singer: "It might be fitting to begin in our survey with the contemporary prototype of the genre, the so called Ideal Jazz Singer, Billie Holiday. Billie's achievements encompass nearly three decades and all seven of our criteria, including a sense of humor so wry, so bitingly sardonic, that no one has successfully been able to imitate it. The quality of her phrasing and inventiveness is such that it cannot be said so assuredly of any other singer that, once she has given her imprint to a song, no one else's version ever sounds quite right, somehow. On hearing Billie's original recording of *What A Little Moonlight Can Do*, it sounds as fresh and stimulating as it did in 1935. Billie's plaintive voice has its roots in searing personal experience; emotion felt and truly reproduced is rarely demonstrated on record as it is on either the Clef or Commodore version of *Strange Fruit*, a classic song of protest."

This is the opinion of many about an artist whose ability was debated for almost ten years. Here we have a period, near the end of her life, of over a year of highly praised performances. Unfortunately, the records of most of these performances, those that were recorded, were released after her death.

♪

Chapter 31

The beginning of 1959, as the end of 1958, was like a resurrection for Billie. That all changed in March of 1959, when Lester Young died and Billie was devastated. They would not let her sing at his funeral and that hurt her deeply. Next to her mother, I think Pres' death pained her the most. She said, "I'll be the next one to go." In May 1959 she performed one number at a benefit at the Phoenix Theater in Greenwich Village. In the middle of her second number she fainted and was taken to the hospital, which friends had been trying to do for weeks. She hated hospitals and probably feared them since she had said many times that she would never go to a hospital. Too, she remembered how her father had died.

George Hoefer, the New York editor of DOWNBEAT, in the July 9, 1959 issue wrote an article entitled: "How Death Came Near For Lady Day." He wrote: "She was under the care of Dr. Eric Caminer. At 2 P.M. on Sunday, May 31, she collapsed as Frankie Freedom, a young singing hopeful and her protégé, was serving her custard and oatmeal, as prescribed by her doctor. She went into a coma after fighting against going to the hospital." Dr. Caminer made arrangements for her to be admitted to Knickerbocker Hospital and called a police ambulance. In New York, you can't get hauled to a hospital without going through the Police Department, unless you want to pay $25 for the trip. At those rates they could haul you to Buffalo. Freedom rode the emergency ambulance to Knickerbocker and waited while Billie lay on a stretcher for more than an hour before any medical attention at all was given to her." According to reporter Bill Dufty, records at the hospital say

Miss Holiday was admitted at 3:40 P.M. After diagnosis as a case of 'drug addiction and alcoholism,' she was put in another ambulance and taken to the Metropolitan Hospital in Harlem, a city institution. In the meantime, Dr. Caminer was on his way to Knickerbocker. When he got there, of course, Billie was gone. So he started for Metropolitan. He knew Billie was in serious trouble with a heart and liver condition. Dr. Caminer finally arrived at Metropolitan at 5:50 P.M. He found his patient lying on a stretcher in the hall, unconscious, unattended and still not hospitalized as the cardiac emergency she was. When he asked for the doctor in charge, he was told, 'He went to dinner.' Dr. Caminer immediately had Billie put into an oxygen tent. There was no question of racial discrimination involved, according to Caminer, for about half the patients and much of the staff at Metropolitan are Negro. 'It might have happened to anybody,' he said. Nobody at either hospital apparently knew that the patient was *the* Lady Day. She was registered as Eleanora McKay, which is her married name. (She is married to her manager, Louis McKay.)"

On June 30, 1959 and July 1, 1959, Douglas Watt wrote a two-page article in the *New York Mirror* called "The Billie Holiday Story" listing the problems that she faced throughout her life. After 46 days in the hospital, Billie Holiday died at 3:10 A.M. on July 17, 1959. She was 44 years old.

Kudos were now coming in from all over the country, and all the things that should have been said when she was alive were being said now. Everyone was looking for someone to replace Billie Holiday. Of course, that was impossible because one cannot supplant a genius. But many can idolize, be influenced by or copy. All three groups came down the line. Ralph J. Gleason, a jazz columnist from San Francisco wrote, "I remember when she opened at Café Society in New York in the winter of 1938-39 for her first big break. She was shocking in her personal magnetism. Standing there with a thin spotlight on her great, sad face and a gardenia in her hair she sang *Strange Fruit* and *Fine and Mellow*, and the singers were never the same thereafter."

And not only jazz critics, but others wrote of our loss. LeRoy Jones, in his book *Black Music*, wrote of Billie: "Nothing was more perfect than she was…More than I have felt to say, she says always…A voice that grew more from a singer's instrument to a woman's. And from that…to a black landscape of need, and perhaps suffocated desire. Sometimes you are afraid to listen to this lady."

Francis Newton in *The New Statesman* wrote: "She was the Puccini heroine among blues singers, or rather among jazz singers…her natural idiom was the pop song. Her unique achievement was to have twisted this into a genuine expression of the major passion by means of a total disregard of its sugary tunes, or indeed of any tune other than her own few delicately crying elongated notes, phrased like Bessie Smith or Louis Armstrong in sack-cloth, sung in a thin, gritty, haunting voice whose natural mood was an unresigned and voluptuous welcome for the pains of love…Suffering was her profession but she did not accept it."

CONFIDENTIAL Magazine, October 1959, with an article, "I Needed Heroin to Live," was sympathetic—the mistakes notwithstanding. Some of the best small newspapers like the Lowell Sun (Massachusetts), July 1959 had "…And Walk Off Singing" by Pertinax, and all the poetry and kind words that she would have loved to hear when she was alive were now being read by those who never cared or cried over her and by those who did. Unfortunately, we immortalize financial success rather than the artistic accomplishments. Jazz Hot from France had a cover picture of Billie and Louis Armstrong from the movie *New Orleans* on the cover with two pages of pictures and comments. Their October issue had five pages of pictures and story. Were there no others to write of what she gave to the world in general and to jazz in particular? Ralph Waldo Emerson said that we never know the gods when they are among us. So it was with Billie and Lester Young in 1959. They both gave so much and got so very little in return.

After her death, a friend of mine wrote to me about Billie at the Phoenix Theater. "She was dressed all in white and wore…her usual gardenias. She had to be helped off the stage in the middle of her second number. I had never seen her before. In spite of the fact that she was sick, there was something beautiful and almost regal about her."

The NEW YORK POST had a five-part series by William Dufty called "The Billie Holiday Story." It is impossible to repeat the articles written about her death and how many mistakes were written as fact. Thankfully, there was Nat Hentoff to write an article for ROGUE Magazine called, "The Last Days of Billie Holiday." In DOWNBEAT,

Leonard Feather wrote a two-page article entitled "Requiescat in Pace."

In August of 1959, the last album that Billie recorded in March of that year for MGM records was released. Reviewing the album, DOWNBEAT wrote, "In spite of everything, Lady Day had it right up to the end. It was like hearing tunes for the first time when Billie sang them, even though you had heard them performed hundreds of times before by others." They gave it four stars. Most of the other critics wrote with various reservations about her voice, but the emotional impact could not be denied by anyone.

In time, many musicians would come to believe and were quoted as saying that they thought the Verve sides were her best. For me, everything she recorded was special. Any singer changes as they get older, but nobody got the bad rap that Billie did. Other singers have lost their voices, gone flat, lost everything that a good singer needs, and no one condemned them to the degree that they condemned Billie. Billie was the kind of performer who was so personal and so universal at the same time. Everybody wanted her to be what she was when they first were dazzled by her genius. If they heard her in the thirties, they wanted her to sound like that forever. She couldn't. She was a jazz singer. If you heard her during the Decca period, then that was what she was expected to sound like forever. The same holds true for the Commodore sides. Only on Verve did they start to seriously dismiss her. Finally, when *Lady in Satin* was released, they really ganged up on her.

But she fooled them all. True art never dies because it is so universal it is left for succeeding generations to understand and enjoy. She was only 44 when she died, which was 50 years ago. In the last 50 years, more people, I would venture to say, are buying her records than people in her own time. Without the racism against jazz, we would have heard her recordings on the radio and "grown up" musically with her. Now it is left for the people who will never see her except on a few feet of film to truly know what a great artist she was – and is. For me she is the singer of the 20th Century. Let's see what this century has to offer.

One summer, I was doing stock at the Williamstown Summer Theater in Massachusetts. When the season was over, I went to New York. I had made a lot of good friends at Williamstown. One was the son of one of my favorite film directors. The son had the choice of plays he wished to see. All he had to do was call and the tickets were waiting. On numerous occasions, he invited me along and in this way I saw four or five plays.

Another friend of mine was doing a play with a group from Columbia University, and she asked if I wanted to be a member of the chorus. The play was *Agamemnon*, and the director was a man who was very hip. He used the recording of *Saeta* from Miles Davis' *Sketches of Spain* album to heighten the return of Agamemnon to Argos. It worked so well. And hearing Miles for two weeks was great. Why there are so few jazz scores for film is beyond me. It is great to hear jazz records, but hearing Duke Ellington's score from *Anatomy of a Murder* was better. John Lewis wrote the score for *No Sun in Venice* and *Odds Against Tomorrow*. And Clint Eastwood frequently uses Lennie Niehaus to score his films. These few examples alone should give filmmakers ample proof that the various styles and moods of jazz can create a truly unique addition to any film.

Chapter 32

Reliving these memories with jazz musicians reminds me of the first time I attended the Newport Jazz Festival in Rhode Island. I was walking around with my friend and bumped into Paul Desmond. I stupidly said, "What are you doing here?" We laughed a lot and talked a little. In California, I used to tell Paul Desmond that I was waiting for him to blow a clinker because he always played so perfectly. As I left, I told him I would like to hear a clinker that evening. Of course, he never blew that clinker. It was a great festival, the music was superb, and walking around talking to the various musicians was intensely enjoyable. This was the 1956 festival when Duke Ellington broke up the festival with his *Diminuendo and Crescendo in Blue*. The crowd went wild while Paul Gonzalves on tenor sax played 27 choruses. People jumped up, screamed and ended up dancing in the aisles. Generally, they went wild.

The second festival I attended was in 1958 and it was the festival that started Anita O'Day's comeback. Satchmo, Monk, Mulligan, Dinah Washington, and all the others who were there performed brilliantly. At midnight, jazz critic, Willis Conover, introduced Mahalia Jackson, the world's greatest gospel singer. The crowd roared as she came on stage. As she started her song, it began to rain. No one left. And they were more than compensated because in a very short time, it stopped raining. She continued to sing over ten songs and they wouldn't let her go. By the time she sang *The Lord's Prayer*, I said to the girl I was with, "Now let someone tell me there is no God."

While I was in New York with the satirical group, Rissa Presents, we played a gallery opening for some modern artists. They asked who could bartend between the two shows, and I said I could. They put me to work for an extra $5. Some people were leaving tips, but the owner of the gallery stopped that fast. I can't understand that. As if it was coming out of his pocket. I thought, "I'm not dumb. I make drinks when people come to the house. Right? Scotch, bourbon, vodka, gin, ouzo, Metaxa. That's easy." Some people began to call for mixed drinks. I told them that I didn't have the ingredients. I used that excuse at other parties. But I also learned to make mixed drinks and became quite good. In time, I was getting calls to go to work for some pretty good places.

When I got back to Los Angeles, I went to file for unemployment. On the way there, I ran into a friend for whom I had done some translations. He never paid me. He said to do it for the "psichi" (soul) of my grandparents. I heard that in New York and told one guy that I had done enough "psihica" (for the souls of) all of my relatives to last two lifetimes.

As it was, I liked this guy because he was funny. I told him what I was doing and he said, "Don't go there. There's a job at this Greek nightclub that is opening next week by some people from Chicago." The owner's name was Jason, so I went to see him and he hired me. I lied about my work experience. I waited a week or so for the remodeling to be completed and nothing happened.

Christmas was coming. I was broke and I was getting nervous. I went to see the owner of the club and they said there would be a delay. They had run out of money. Through a friend, I got a job at a small neighborhood bar, and it gave me the chance to learn to make more drinks.

In California, I also used the "we don't have the ingredient" routine. I got by OK until some guy said, "You have gin, don't you?" "Yes". "You have lemon juice and sugar or sweet and sour mix?" "Yes". "You have soda water?" "Yes". "Then why can't you make a Tom Collins?" I said, "Oh, I'm sorry. We don't make them that way in New York." So I made him a Collins and he loved it. Then the Greek club opened. As for the Greek nightclub, I figured all they would drink was ouzo and Metaxa brandy or a glass of retsina wine. Man, was I mistaken!

What helped me most was that many friends would come in and order all kinds of mixed drinks. In that way, I learned more drinks, and it became easier at night when the heavy crowd came in after nine or ten to get the drinks made without looking in the Bartender's Guide. I was making great tips because I had girls at the bar so men would come in and stay when they saw the girls. So to impress the girls, they left bigger tips. This all came about in a very unusual way.

A lot of girls I knew said that they had heard that Greek men make the best husbands and would I please introduce them to my Greek friends. I told the girls to come and I told the guys to come, and I built a great bar business. It was also good for the house because the Greek clubs had very little business early. And my little "mating service" ran from about six to nine. I did get a few couples together who got married and are still married! I should have been a marriage broker!

Since my job was a night job, I could go on auditions on the days that I wasn't sleeping on the beach. The club was booming. A great musician who played the bouzouki was hired, but he would only play when he felt like it. Sometimes he wouldn't play at all. He'd be social and sit with the women—married or not. Yes, there were quite a few fights. Mostly though it was great because there were Greeks, Jews, Turks, Armenians, Syrians, Lebanese, Americans, and we were friends! One night when the bouzouki player decided to play, he did a mini concert, which lasted until 4 A.M. He had gotten up on the stand at 2 A.M. when most of the people were leaving and no drinks could be served. When he started to play, about half of the crowd returned. His opening was a "taksim" which is totally improvised. It was out of this world. I was pleased in later years to see that he had done an album with Phil Woods, the great alto sax player called *Greek Cooking*. Liner notes by the great Nat Hentoff.

♪

Chapter 33

DOWNBEAT Magazine, February 1, 1962, had a sketch of Billie Holiday on the cover, which stated, "Billie Holiday—The Voice of Jazz," and proceeded to explain in four full pages why. The article was by Leonard Feather who said, "To call Billie the voice of jazz is logical, for no matter what controversies raged around other singers' relationships to jazz, it could never be disputed that whether she sang a ballad, Tin Pan Alley potboiler, or the national anthem, Billie remained inescapably a pure jazz sound."

Later on in the article, he wrote: "Billie didn't live to see herself voted into first place in a DOWNBEAT readers' poll. To some observers, this may seem insignificant, yet it is meaningful in the light of the facts about others who were more fortunate. The jazz fans who voted for their favorite jazz singers in 1942 elected Helen Forrest, and in 1943 Jo Stafford. In 1944, probably Billie's peak year musically and commercially, they chose Dinah Shore. That's the way things were in those days, not just in jazz polls but in American life, and it would be naïve not to acknowledge that this didn't have something to do with making Billie Holiday what she was."

And further on in the article: "The Holiday concert memorial album, with the Gilbert Millstein narration, has been lying on my desk for two months, and I still can't quite bring myself to play it. But I would like to believe that all who voted Billie into the Hall of Fame (two months earlier in the December 21, 1961 issue of DOWNBEAT) and all who didn't, but are willing to believe just a little of what I have said about her, will listen with open hearts. Perhaps you will hear some of what I heard during the years when, for me and for so many others of our time, Billie's was the most moving human voice on earth."

From ESQUIRE's 1947 Yearbook of Jazz:

When Dinah Shore went to Milt Gabler's Commodore Music Shop for help concerning a "blues" that she was scheduled to sing on the "Society of Lower Basin Street" program which had recently signed her, he locked her in a booth for a couple of hours with a stack of Bessie Smith, Lee Wiley and Billie Holiday records. A few weeks later Dinah introduced a new song on the program called *Mad About Him, Sad About Him Blues.* And that's how Dinah learned some blues.

One night, a friend and I went to a jazz club in Greenwich Village to see Thelonius Monk. We waited for 45 minutes. Finally, he arrived. He was wearing one of his famous hats and looked very cool as he sat down at the piano. He hesitated for a few moments, and then hit one key on the piano. It was obvious that he did not like what he heard. So he got up and left. Many people condemned him as they had condemned Miles Davis for turning his back on his audience while he was playing at the Storyville Club in Boston. They were wrong to condemn. In Monk's case, the piano was not well tuned. In Miles' case, the monitors were placed in such a position that he was obliged to turn in order to better hear himself. Many other musicians have done things that seem either arrogant or unprofessional or both. In most cases which concern jazz musicians, the reasons for the seemingly odd behavior was a desire to play in such a way that it would not only please the audience but please the musicians themselves.

Chapter 34

For a period of time, I worked as a bartender for one of the top caterers in town. On one particular night, I was working at a party at the home of one of our greatest songwriters. It was a New Year's party and one of the guests was Rosemary Clooney. I was so busy that I couldn't get to her until they said that dinner would be served in 10 minutes. Everybody started going to the restrooms. Fortunately, the hostess waited until all the visits to the restrooms were made and then still gave them some more time. Rosemary Clooney was one of the last to go to the restroom. As she passed me, I went up to her and told her my story with Billie and we got to talking. I had her by the wrist without knowing what I was doing, but I wanted so much to tell her how much I enjoyed her tribute album to Billie called *Here's to My Lady* (this was about 10 years after Billie died). I told her that the LP with Duke Ellington was a classic and I still think that. Although not a jazz singer, her influences are deeply rooted in jazz. She started to step back but I never pulled my hand away from hers. In time, the idiot that I am, I realized that she wanted to go to the restroom and I was keeping her. I let her wrist go and apologized, and she said something about understanding because she, too, loved Billie the way that I did. My closing line was to repeat how happy Billie was every night at Jazz City when she received the gardenias that Rosie and Jose Ferrer had sent. Rosie was a great lady and she, too, is now gone. A great loss. Her Concord recordings attest to her singing greatness and the variety of tunes that she could sing and sing well.

One day when I was lying in the sun and sand of State Beach at the end of Sunset Boulevard and reading the Hollywood trade papers, I jumped up and said to my friends: "Linda Darnell is doing a film in Greece and I'm going to do it." I didn't know how, but I was determined. It was to be shot in Greece on the island of Kos in the Eastern Mediterranean group of islands called the Dodecanese. It is the island where Hippocrates, the Father of Medicine, was born in 460 B.C. There is a tree there under which Hippocrates is said to have taught medicine. It is about 2,500 years old. In the center, are the petrified remains of the original tree and surrounding it like ripples in a pool are the various barks of trees that have grown there through the ages. It has a wrought-iron fence around its 48-foot circumference. I was dying to go there but my agent could not get me an audition.

I found out that Linda Darnell would be appearing in Las Vegas at one of the hotels. She had broken in her act at the Shamrock Hotel in Houston, Texas. In the interim, I had found out that there was a part for someone to play her brother. It was to be a modern love story of a Greek Orthodox girl and an Italian Roman Catholic who desire to marry. The plan is thwarted by her brother. Raf Vallone was hired for the part of the Italian. I wrote her a letter. She answered me and invited me to go to Las Vegas to meet with her. I had, naturally, sent her my picture and my resume with the letter. I didn't have a car and I thought I'd have to fly. This meant borrowing money, but fate knocked on my door and some friends came to visit who had recently moved to California from New Hampshire. During the course of their visit, we discussed the film and the above-mentioned particulars and they offered me their car. What a break!

I drove to Vegas and met Linda Darnell. It was about one hour before she went on. I can still remember her beauty. A knockout. Her coloring and her porcelain skin which was flawless. She liked my "Greek" look and hired me. We talked about the film, when we would be leaving and that she would call me when the time came to sign the contracts. I knew my break had come. A film in Greece, a third starring role and, hopefully, a good career doing a film I had dreamed of doing. About a month later her secretary called me and told me we would be leaving in three weeks and that the details would be forthcoming. Did I have my passport? I had everything.

I gave notice to my job and was flying high. In less than two weeks, someone else called to tell me what I had already learned—that

Linda Darnell had died in a fire in Chicago. I saw it later on the news. At the time, she was going with a Greek doctor from Chicago. I was upset about the film, but my main sorrow was for her. She had been through so much. The words to use in explaining her beauty and her kindness are not in my vocabulary. And I shall always remember her films, especially *A Letter to Three Wives*. I watch it whenever it's on TV (as well as anything else that Joe Mankiewitz either directed and/or wrote). Linda Darnell is one of those bittersweet memories that I can never quite lose.

♪

Chapter 35

Then another joy! Columbia Records released a three-LP set of their Billie Holiday's records from the 1930s. DOWNBEAT, HI-FI, STEREO REVIEW, LIFE Magazine, THE NEW YORKER and dozens more all agreed on the greatness of these sides. For me, it was a little difficult to get used to some of these sides. I grew up on the few Columbias but mostly on the Decca sides, and even though Columbia was not my era, her genius won me over. When the second three-LP set came out, it received the same rave reviews. It was like growing up when these sides were first being released. True art can do that!

Then they started talking about her again. Everywhere people were looking for the "next" Billie Holiday, as if there could ever be another like her. In ESQUIRE magazine, September 1964, music critic David Newman in reviewing some new recordings said: "I'd like to point out, finally, that it is possible to project drama and feeling and even pain without falling into all this manneristic anxiety. The pity is, Billie Holiday isn't around any longer to show them how it's done." Billie was sorely missed.

Being an artist in America is very unfair. In jazz, it's even more unfair. Every decade or so some flash in the pan will come on the scene and claim, or their managers will claim, that this is a jazz artist. They do a lot of PR and get them television work and record deals. So they are called "jazz" players or singers. They win jazz polls and sell many records and make money and then, after a short time, they are never heard from again.

During the time that the pseudo or quasi-jazz musicians are getting all the press and all the club dates, the true ARTIST is struggling to earn a living. Some make it, barely, and some leave the business, and, if they're lucky, they'll be playing gigs around their hometowns or they'll be janitors or window washers as has happened to two giants of jazz. The very lucky ones will be sought out by fans that have just discovered them and help to bring them back into the public eye. Even then, they may not be acknowledged. The sadness sometimes is that some never return to the scene. And for most jazz fans, that is our loss. Thankfully, some have left great recordings to speak for them. That's all we can hope for in jazz.

I continued working as a bartender. This time, in downtown Los Angeles where all the stockbrokers ate and drank. While I was there, I was up for a pilot and a part in another movie. I wanted the pilot so badly that I was constantly on the phone with my agent. I got two callbacks. But with my luck you may have already guessed it. I didn't get the job. I just settled down and kept working as a bartender and auditioning. When being asked what I was doing on the phone, I told them that I was looking for another job. Back then you never told anyone that you were an actor, because if you did, they wouldn't hire you. If you ever wanted to take off, they would assume you got an acting job and then they would fire you. So you never told anyone. One of the bartenders asked me, "What kind of job?" And the other bartender said, "I thought you were a bookie with all those calls".

There had been talk about a movie on the life of Lady Day since her death, but nothing ever happened and for many reasons. Then, in 1972, a film called *Lady Sings the Blues* and supposedly based on her autobiography was released. It was the worst kind of rehashed trash with all the misconceptions and distortions usually found in films about famous people. There was no mention of Lester Young or Teddy Wilson. At the very least, these two men should have been depicted. Forget that practically every great jazz man alive played with her and recorded with her. But the aforementioned two, Pres and Teddy, should certainly have been mentioned.

And there were also the plays. TIME Magazine wrote: "...a theatrical fury of interest in the rugged life of Billie Holiday, the supreme jazz singer who died of cumulative effects of dope and despair in 1959.

Brooklyn's Chelsea Theater last week presented a jazz musical called *Lady Day* that uses Holiday (sung by Cecelia Norfleet) as a symbol of the ravages that racial repression can work. 'Seething with anger, this Lady Day misses all that was funny and spunky in the real woman,' said TIME's Drama Critic, T.E. Kalen."

The Hollywood version of the Holiday story is no better. A spindly, cliché-ravaged tale of the sorrow of show biz, *Lady Sings the Blues* stars Diana Ross, former lead singer of the Supremes...it is eerie to watch and listen to Miss Ross, work her way through such songs as *Strange Fruit* and *God Bless the Child*...what she doesn't have is the passion...Billie Holiday, as an artist, deserves a far better memorial.

NEWSWEEK Magazine's Jack Kroll called the play *Lady Day* "...a strange and exasperating production..." and the movie as "Hollywood hokum, a clumsy parade of clichés and stereotypes that seeps venality, cynicism and ineptitude from every sprocket hole."

Chapter 36

The tribute albums were still coming out. Helen Merrill recorded one in Japan with Teddy Wilson. Anita O'Day, as well as many jazz musicians, extolled the virtues of the Japanese jazz fans. In addition, there is a Japanese singer named Kimiko Kasai who recorded an album with Mal Waldron, one of Billie's accompanists. She does credit to Billie's classics: *Lover Man* and *Don't Explain* are exceptionally moving. She does not imitate Billie but she does have the right mood for each song.

By this time, all of the Columbia records had been released, as well as the Decca and most of the Verves. And everyone was finding a "new" Billie Holiday around every corner. Somehow, she never showed up. And all singers were being compared to her. They, too, were jazz singers, and they, too, had "suffered" like Billie as if that is what made her great. Peggy Lee, whom I had met and who was one of the singers influenced by both Billie and Lee Wiley, was one of my favorites, too. But someone wrote how Peggy Lee had suffered as much as Billie. I answered that story with a letter, which the LOS ANGELES TIMES printed, and I quote:

> "Dear Sirs:
>
> I thoroughly enjoy John Hallowell's writing ("Peggy Lee Is Very Different From You and Me," April 12), but he makes a grave mistake when he compares Peggy Lee and her roots to Billie Holiday and her roots. Either he is too young to know Billie's life or he is unaware of what it means to be born

illegitimate, poor and black in a society where you would never be fully accepted simply because you were black. And in 1915 to boot!

Gene Chronopoulos, Los Angeles"

I never knew that so many people read the letters to the editor in newspapers. I don't. So it was left for my friend Chrissie to tell me. (She is one of the five typists who worked on this memoir.) There were many other calls from friends and I was truly surprised and I was pleased. I said, "Run out and buy one of Billie's LPs." I had been collecting articles, record reviews and anything else that pertained to Billie. When I came back from a six-month trip to Greece and other European countries, I was unemployed. I went and bought a 14 x 17 inch clear plastic scrapbook with 50 double plastic pages. I filled it with all the reviews, printed material, and pictures. To this day, friends send me articles from various magazines and newspapers. I no longer save anything simply because her name is printed in it. But I do save the major articles, and though there are not as many, they are all glowing tributes to the genius of Lady Day. And there are more references to her in a variety of books about other people and subjects.

Mal Waldron, who was her pianist in the last years of her life, recorded an album entitled *Left Alone*. It is a fitting tribute to Billie and to Waldron himself.

Webster Young and Paul Quinichette also did a tribute album called *For Lady*, and they captured her mood and feeling to the extent that at times you could almost hear Lady come in for a couple of bars. Dexter Gordon on tenor sax recorded *Don't Explain* and Stanley Turrentine also on tenor sax recorded *God Bless the Child*.

As for me, I got an agent. I lost an agent. He died. I got a new agent who was sleeping on the job. A job here and a job there. I was doing Little Theater work in Los Angeles but still I had to work to pay for my car, my apartment and such. It was a sad period for me because the joy of hunting for classic jazz records by Billie and others was changing rapidly.

As stated previously, since the day that Billie died, there were all these other singers whose managers and agents were telling everyone,

"Here's the new Billie Holiday." That could never happen because Billie was an original. In time, the very respected and intelligent Ralph Gleason started writing reviews about the club dates in San Francisco of Carmen McRae and claimed that she was coming into her own as a major jazz singer.

Carmen has said that she followed Billie Holiday's approach to lyrics and Anita O'Day had followed Billie's lead in improvising the music. Both recorded tribute albums to Lady Day: Carmen in 1962 and Anita in 1991.

A couple of years later, I was sitting at the bar at Jazz City on Carmen McRae's pre-opening night. Carmen was rehearsing and Anita O'Day, who had just finished her engagement that night, was sitting at the bar digging Carmen rehearsing. The place was almost empty and I had stayed to talk to Anita and Carmen and had the added joy of watching the latter rehearse. Naturally, I went to Carmen's opening the next night. I had also thrived on Anita O'Day's comeback at the Newport Jazz Festival in 1958. Since she played L.A. on a regular basis, I saw her many times at the Vine Street Bar and Grill and she always played to packed houses. As for Carmen McRae, the next time I saw her was at the Hong Kong Bar in Century City in Los Angeles. At one of her sets there, she made mention of the fact that she tried to do one of Billie's tunes in every set. Ralph J. Gleason was right. By this time, Carmen had truly become a major jazz singer and her recorded output was extraordinary. Both of these ladies remained in the top ranks of jazz singers for decades. I really miss those small jazz clubs where you could see and hear the artists up close (No standing around five miles away waving candles).

♪

Chapter 37

At the Greek nightclubs where I worked as a bartender, there was really no business until 9 P.M. when the music started. I had to be there at six for the few early dinners we had or for the Greek guys coming from the racetrack to shower me with money--or to ask for a loan. They knew they could come in and eat when they had lost because I had been there many, many times. Remember? One day, when I came into work, the opening waitress said that she had just two ladies who were eating and would I watch them while she went back to put on "a new face." She was always late and always used the same line. So she went back and I looked over. The ladies were eating and didn't look up to ask for anything, so I went back to my opening duties. In time, "Miss New Face" came back and went over to the table. She came back to the bar and brought me a credit card to pay for the ladies' check. I ran the card through the machine and looked at it to see if it printed well. When I saw the name I screamed "Carmen McRae!" I ran over to the table and Carmen was there with Della Reese. I was so excited. I talked to them and when we discussed Billie's film biography, Carmen and I both agreed that we despised the movie *Lady Sings the Blues*. She actually walked out of the movie because she could not stand the lies. She and Billie were very close and Billie had also recorded one of Carmen's compositions. I asked Carmen about any new recordings, and she told me that she had no recording contract at that time. But she was hoping and waiting. I thought of all the great jazz artists who were then or were at other times in the same position. I remember at one point, that pianist Oscar Peterson had not recorded anything for almost seven years. Carmen said, "I've got a lot I'd like to say," meaning a new recording contract. In time, she did release album after album of great jazz on various labels.

For me, every time I saw Billie Holiday it was a source of great joy. But what I felt was her best in-person performance, was when I saw her at a little club called the Waldorf Cellar on Main Street in downtown Los Angeles. It was in the late fifties. It only held about 40 or 50 people, but there were only about four people when we walked in. I had gone with my sister, Kiki. We walked into the club and just about four steps into it, there was a Dutch door to our right. The top door was open and there she stood - Lady Day. Big hellos, greetings and amenities and catching up with her life and career. I told her that I had written a letter about her, which was printed in DOWNBEAT, but that they had cut it down to nothing. They lost the whole essence of the letter. She told me to go home and get it. I told her that I didn't have a car and that it would take me over two hours to go and come back by bus. She said that she would pay for a cab, but after further discussions we thought it would take too long and I didn't want to miss her first set. So we stayed and talked. She had a new Chihuahua called Pepito. She had gotten him at an auction and she said, "Some bitch was bidding against me. She went up to $300." Billie said, "I can't afford $300. Who is that bitch? So I looked over and walked toward her and it was Ava Gardner. 'Hey bitch,' I said, 'I can't afford $300.' So she said, 'Lady, I'm sorry, I didn't know it was you.'

"So, Ava bought it and gave it to me as a gift," said Billie. She told us that she had introduced Ava to Frank Sinatra so they were all friends. She told us that she had told Sinatra to bend his notes and not sing so "flat" (meaning straight). When that part of the conversation was over, Kiki asked Billie, "Is Ava really that beautiful?"

Billie said, "She ain't no prettier than you are, honey."

We laughed and Kiki slapped Billie lightly on the back and said,

"Oh, Billie, you are such a riot."

That slap was heard around the room because Billie's gown was backless. Thankfully, there weren't more people there or somebody would think she was beating up on Billie. We teased Kiki for months after I told all our friends. "Why did you beat up on Billie?" "I thought you liked her." "Did Gene beat up on you for that?" She heard it all. By this time, Billie had become a very important part of my life.

The place had about four other people come in. That's about four people who worked there. Eight customers and I were thinking, here was the world's greatest jazz singer with no audience to speak of.

She never sounded better than that night. After five songs, she went into another song, and without thinking, I yelled out, *"Porgy!"* Billie stopped singing, looked at her piano player and said, *"Porgy."* The piano cut the intro and went into *Porgy* at Billie's signal. I felt embarrassed but Billie smiled at me. Then she sang *Ain't Nobody's Business* among another half dozen songs - which made it the best set ever. But it was also true that "Spinning a piece of vinyl cannot be considered a substitute for the electric experience of watching and feeling Billie sing from the tips of her fingers," as Richard Hadlock said in DOWNBEAT's 1960 Yearbook.

In retrospect, this episode leaves me with a very sad feeling. The club was in downtown Los Angeles when it was beginning to feel the impact of too many people in one area. It was, I think, the beginning of homeless people in such large numbers. The club had become a little more than a dive, but Billie made it sparkle.

Chapter 38

I introduced a lot of people to jazz, but no one took it up as much as my nephew and godson, Yanni. He was my sister's son and had listened to Billie through the years. At a large record store, while we were looking at the new CD releases, he came across a 12-CD set of all live performances by Billie. They were packaged three CDs to a box. Each box was $50. I wasn't going to get it, but he said to me, "My godfather always said, 'If you find something you like, buy it. If you have no money, charge it.'" He did that himself. So out came my credit card, and I have never regretted that purchase. There are things there that are fantastic. Since then, I have never seen those same boxed sets, which were from Italy. This set was also a source of information as to where most of Billie's bootleg recordings had come from. Most of these had come from nightclubs, and radio broadcasts. There are, in this collection, numerous examples of Billie's fearless and daring improvisations. For once, I followed my own advice. Thanks to my godson.

It is common knowledge that Leonard Feather came here from England initially just to meet and interview Billie Holiday. They were friends for years. He was instrumental in getting a star for Billie Holiday on Hollywood Boulevard. It took a long time. After the release of *Lady Sings the Blues*, a movie that should be ashamed of itself, a renewed interest into the life and recordings of that genius came about. A short article by Leonard Feather in the LOS ANGELES TIMES should give ample proof of his frustration that Feather and thousands of others felt. From the Sunday, December 27, 1982 LOS ANGELES TIMES: "Irony of the Year": "It was reported last week that stars will be implanted in

Hollywood's 'Walk of Fame' for Diana Ross and Billy Dee Williams, who were seen in the *Lady Sings the Blues* movie that grossly distorted the life of Billie Holiday, one of the century's great creative artists; yet another year has gone by without any word about a posthumous star for Holiday herself. (Mayor Bradley, have you forgotten our talk two years ago, when you assured me you would look into this?)" Finally, in 1986 a star for Billie Holiday was put on Vine Street, just a block south of Hollywood Boulevard through the donations of friends of Lady Day.

Her star should have been on Hollywood Boulevard in a more prestigious setting while those who she influenced had stars on the Boulevard. I attended the ceremony and listened to the music and heard the speeches. As stated earlier, Singer Annie Ross said, "Every lady singer should get down on her knees and thank God that there was a Billie Holiday." Rosemary Clooney said that the addition of Billie Holiday's star "adds luster to all the others who had stars before now." Carmen McRae said that Billie could take a "dumb song" and make it "palatable." Actor Jose Ferrer said he was in awe of Billie because she was "one of the very few artists who had an absolutely original talent." Marla Gibbs said, "I feel she was born out of love, suffered for lack of love and died for want of love." When viewing these people on CBS, NBC and local Los Angeles KTLA Channel 5, I have seen the name Holiday spelled with two "L's," McRae spelled with a "Mac." Errors like saying that Billie Holiday was named Lady by her fans and "Billie died of an overdose." Minor things? If it were the first hundred times, OK. But Billie's name has been misspelled and facts about her have been distorted thousands of times. For an artist who was around for over 20 years in the public eye, that is disgraceful. On the local Channel 5, the narrator said lovely things about Billie, including, "She was forgotten by those who should not have forgotten; when others were being honored in Hollywood, she was not."

During the end of this statement, the camera cut back to Frank Sinatra's star on the Boulevard. For me, a bad cut. Sinatra always admired Billie's timing, phrasing and the deep feeling of her lyrics. In 1958, in EBONY Magazine, Sinatra said, "With few exceptions, every major pop singer in the United States during her generation has been touched in some way by her genius. It is Billie Holiday whom I first heard in 52nd Street clubs in the early Thirties, who was, and still remains, the greatest single musical influence on me." I don't know why they cut it that way, but it looked bad. Billie herself liked Sinatra very much and told me so on at least two occasions. Was it intentional? I don't know. It was taken that way by some of my friends.

Speaking of EBONY magazine, here is a letter I sent to them. It was never published. It was in response to an article they printed on the greatest moments in black musical history.

Letters to the Editor
Ebony Magazine
820 So. Michigan Avenue
Chicago, IL 60605

July 9, 2000

While it is true that you could have listed one thousand great moments in black musical history, it saddens me to see the name of many geniuses missing from your list. But for the moment let me bemoan the fact that the name of Billie Holiday is missing. Her arrival on the scene in the mid-thirties was the beginning of modern jazz singing. For the first time in jazz, a singer was not just a singer. Billie improvised the music just as a jazz musician did. And she never lost sight of the lyric. As a result, the jazz musicians with whom she had sung loved her. This kind of relationship was missing with other singers. She influenced them and they influenced her. Primarily with Lester Young's backing, she defined the modern jazz singer who could sing on, after, before, and over the beat but in the end, she always came out right on the beat. It is, as you say, true that all phases of American music have been influenced by black music and this continues today. More than any other singer and as much as most jazz instrumentalists, Billie Holiday has influenced singers and instrumentalists.

Ralph Waldo Emerson said that, "We never know the gods when they are among us." So it is with Lady Day. With Billie, they tried to bury her ten years before her time. And by her own admission, it took audiences ten years to even know what she was doing.

Today, there are critics and others who dismiss her except for those early sides with Lester Young. All of Billie's records on Decca, Commodore, Verve and the last two on MGM and Columbia show us an artist who through her honesty and complete artistry can express every human emotion in all its complexity, in a voice so unique it has never been duplicated.

Thankfully her influence is felt today in practically all the singers who came after her.

Gene Chronopoulos
Los Angeles, CA

♪

Chapter 39

In closing, I am reprinting a part of the oath that Alexander the Great made in 324 B.C.

You might ask why and rightly so. The reason is that jazz has never become our popular music because of all the racism and negative rap that it has received through the years. Had the world learned the value of Alexander's oath, perhaps jazz would be as popular here as it is in other places in the world. Since I believe in the axiom "Better Late Than Never," I give you that oath.

"Now that the wars are coming to an end, I wish you to prosper in peace. May all the mortals from now on live like one people, in concord and for mutual advancement.

"Consider the world as your country, with laws common to all and where the best will govern, irrespective of tribe. I do not distinguish among men, as the narrow-minded do, both among Greeks and barbarians. I am not interested in the descent of the citizens, nor their racial origins. I classify them using only one criterion: virtue.

"For me every virtuous foreigner is a Greek and every evil Greek worse than a barbarian. If differences ever develop between you, never have recourse to arms, but solve them peacefully. If necessary, I shall be your arbitrator.

"You must not consider God like an autocratic despot, but as a common father of all, so that your behavior may resemble the life siblings have in a family.

"On my part, I shall consider you all equal, whites or blacks, and I wish you would be not only subject of the commonwealth, but participants and partners.

"As much as this depends on me, I shall try to bring about what I promised. The oath we made over tonight's libations, hold onto like a contract of love.

"The Leader"

That was 2,300 years ago and we still have not learned that all of us are, in fact, brothers and sisters.

Epilogue

When I started writing this memoir, I simply pulled out the large scrapbook that I have kept through the years on the career of Billie Holiday. It now has over 80 pages. I went through it page by page and in this way was able to remember many things that I would have probably forgotten.

The last page has the picture that I took with Billie at Jazz City in Hollywood and a few record reviews from some of the tribute albums recorded in her honor. Since there is no more room in the book for more items on Billie, I have gathered all of them and have put them into a large envelope, which is tucked in the leaf of the back cover of the scrapbook.

I didn't write this to show that I'm in any way an expert on jazz. My joy lies in the fact that I discovered jazz and its artists and the influence they had on me.

There are, of course, various bulletins from the jazz record clubs in which you will find practically everything that she ever recorded.

The complete Columbia sides on 10 CDs with a 116-page booklet.

The complete Commodore sides with a 40-page booklet.

The complete Decca sides with a 36-page booklet.

The complete Verve sides on 10 CDs with a 220-page booklet.

The few sides that remain on smaller labels you will have to find on your own. Discover the joy of discovering jazz, our own truly American art form. It will bring you pleasure for years to come.

I once read that Thelonious Monk had tacked a picture of Billie Holiday onto his ceiling at which he stared. I did the same thing. So every night I looked up at my picture of Billie and said, "God bless you, Lady, 'cause you got your own."

About the Author

Gene Chronopoulos was born and raised in New Hampshire. He attended Los Angeles City College where he pursued a career in music and film. He works today as an actor and director of numerous live musical theatrical productions in Los Angeles and has a strong interest in the history of jazz.

Why I wrote this book:

Having traveled to many foreign countries, all of them were well aware and knowledgeable that Jazz was America's music You heard it in stores, hotels, and taxi cabs. Unfortunately, here, in the country of its birth, it's not as respected as it is around the world. There are many reasons for this, all of them shameful. It would be to our credit to embrace the only art form that we have given to the world.

The following quotes, favorites of the author, were chosen after a complimentary copy of the manuscript was distributed to a select group of readers.

QUOTES

"A terrific personal account about the early jazz age. A great entertaining book about the singers and musicians that made it happen. A Real Winner"

-Mike Connors - Actor
Television's "Mannix"

****

"Gene Chronopoulos invites you into his magical youth and his wonderful discovery of jazz - especially the music and stylings of the great jazz singer Billie Holiday. Gene was lucky enough to have lived in a time when celebrities were more real and accessible and music was sought after and appreciated. It was fascinating and illuminating to read about so many jazz greats, shared by someone who was really there, watching jazz history unfold. These were real people playing their gigs, singing their songs, dealing with club owners and audiences, all the while creating America's greatest music. I also enjoyed reading the tidbits of Gene's Greek culture sprinkled throughout the stories.

When Billie Holiday was receiving bad press and too much focus on her substance use and not enough praise for her incomparable jazz singing, it's admirable that Gene took the time on many occasions to write directly to the newspapers and magazines to stand up for her as an artist.

As a one of a kind jazz singer, Billie Holiday influenced her own contemporaries such as Ella Fitzgerald, Sarah Vaughn, Chet Baker and countless others as well as paving the way for all jazz singers and musicians to come in every generation. After reading this captivating book, Gene's knowledge and enthusiasm for jazz have given me a new appreciation and reverence for 'Lady Day', her music and her life."

- Jazz singer Krisanthi Pappas